Praise for
No Longer Untouchable

"Sarah Davison-Tracy's *No Longer Untouchable* is a beautiful, heart-wrenching depiction of the realities for some of the most vulnerable—the women and girls of the *Badi* communities in Nepal. Told in their own words and with great attention to detail, this book honors the horrors of sex trafficking and the unexpected hope and strength evident in these survivors. Davison-Tracy captures the culture, emotion, abuse, and journey of each woman with artful storytelling that connects an overwhelming, complex issue with the real people it affects.

"And yet, despite the darkness, hope and light are woven through every chapter, every story. *No Longer Untouchable* is an essential read for those who need real-life inspiration, for anyone interested in human trafficking's impact, and for readers who need a reminder that heroes can rise from ashes."

–Laura Parker,
Co-founder and President of The Exodus Road

"Sarah Davison-Tracy has written a compelling exposé of sex trafficking in Nepal and India by sharing the heartbreaking stories of five young survivors. I read the whole book in one sitting. We must work together to end this atrocious industry."

–Vaun Swanson,
President of Daya International

"I stand in awe of these young women's courage, strength, and tenacity. It is more than a book on human rights and sex trafficking. It is a story of the triumph of the human spirit and of the greatness that can be achieved when a group of people come together to fight for one another."

–Jessica Muñoz,
President and Founder of Ho'ola Na Pua

No Longer Untouchable gives a sobering and hopeful view into one of the most urgent challenges that faces our world today."

–Drew Edwards,
Co-founder of Pangea Educational Development

"Sarah Davison-Tracy and these extraordinary storytellers take readers on an unbelievable journey into the terrifying and oppressive world of sex trafficking. And yet, they somehow led me to a story ending with more hope than I ever thought possible. This is a must-read for anyone committed to a life of difference-making and connecting more deeply with those around them."

–Sarah Jackson,
Founder of Casa de Paz

"In this heartfelt and compelling book, Sarah Davison-Tracy shines a light on the unimaginable suffering of young Nepali women forced to be sex slaves. Her depiction of 'a day in the life' is the beginning of an urgently needed global conversation to help empower communities to break the chains of human trafficking."

–Sarah Symons,
Founder of Her Future Coalition

"These stories are moving, shocking, and anger-forming all at once. These are the stories we need to hear. These are the atrocities we need to see, the fact that discrimination and oppression of women are still happening to such an extent in certain parts of our world. We need these stories; we need these women's voices. This is the time for these stories to be heard because none of us are free while even one of us is enslaved. The writing immediately pulls you in and takes you into their lives. It's a reading that renders you lost in time. Time stands still as you immerse yourself within these pages; this is a book that is both a call to awaken and to intervene. Every justice fighter and freedom seeker, changemaker and world-shaper should have this book in their library."

–Lauren Jacobs,
Desmond Tutu Prize Winner,
Author, and Social Justice Journalist

"Get ready to FEEL! *No Longer Untouchable* will move and disturb you in the best way. Sarah Davison-Tracy and her team of powerful storytellers have done a masterful job opening a door to a world many would prefer to keep shut."

–Rochelle Raimão,
Independent Film Producer

"Sarah Davison-Tracy's *No Longer Untouchable* is a painful, devastating, and incredibly inspiring book. It's a necessary read, plain and simple.

"By helping these brave *Badi* women document what should never be allowed to take place anywhere, at any time, on this planet, Sarah Davison-Tracy allows these women access to something more valuable than any amount of money or resources could bring—*dignity in being heard*. Emotions of every sort came over me as I turned the pages—anger, horror, and profound sadness.

"But the book doesn't leave you there in this dark spot. The courage we discover through their words has a very important effect—it awakens a sort of primal call to respond to this injustice—to stop it. The bravery required to share these intimate and horrifying experiences makes you want to *do* something. It makes you think if these brave women had the strength to live and tell this hell, we can find our own power and strength to stand by them, to take whatever action, large or small, against it happening anymore."

–Lydia Dean, co-founder of GoPhilanthropic Foundation,
Founder of GoPhilanthropic Travel, and
author of *Jumping the Picket Fence*
and *Light Through the Cracks*

"While reading *No Longer Untouchable*, I kept thinking of the directive, 'Consider the lily.' This call to attend to the intricate details of a common flower seems to be the precursor for us to look up and see our sister, our brother. *If I am moved by the beauty of a lily, I am deeply moved as I consider Hannah, Meena, Aasha, Sakhira, and Khushi.* Their stories are told so well here, and I am grateful to know them. Their courage gives me courage. It is hope in the individual story that keeps hope alive in me that we might see the end of human trafficking."

–Sara Groves, Singer and Songwriter,
Artist Advocate for International Justice Mission

NO LONGER
untouchable

A Story of Human Trafficking, Heroism, and Hope

You! — all — are loved. ♡
xo, Sarah

SARAH DAVISON-TRACY
Foreword by Devisara "Hannah" Badi

No Longer Untouchable:
A Story of Human Trafficking, Heroism, and Hope
Published by Ignite Publishers
Denver, CO

ISBN: 978-09997212-3-0

SOCIAL SCIENCE / Prostitution & Sex Trade

Cover design by Donna Cunningham / Beaux Arts
Editing by Donna Mazzitelli / Writing With Donna
Interior design by Veronica Yager / YellowStudios

IGNITE!
PUBLISHERS

To Hannah, Meena, Aasha, Sakhira, and Khushi.
May your *unstoppable* courage,
unquenchable hope,
and commitment to *unabashedly* love God
and all those you meet
ignite and inspire the hearts, minds, and spirits of many.

Your forever sister,
–Sarah *didi*

Foreword

This
book
should
never
have
been
written.

Although this is true, and before I dive into my passion for this project, let me back up a moment. I'd like to begin with a greeting. This is how I would say hello to you if we met on my streets of Kathmandu.

Namaste, my sister.

Jaimasi, my brother.

I am overwhelmed and honored that today you are holding *our story* in your hands. If you saw me now, you'd see the gleam of joy and excitement in my eyes, with a touch of awe and disbelief, that this book has been published at long last.

And yet, like I said, there are many who did not think this book *could* or *should* be published and many powerful people who *never wanted* it to see the light of day.

To have an entire book written about us in English for the world to read—well, it's never been done before.

In fact, I am persuaded that *this story* will make history.

I believe this book will be like a bomb going off in my country and around the world—a bomb of truth that tells tales that many have worked hard to keep silent and hidden … things like the dark and insidious sources of my people's great suffering and poverty; the ways that, even today, the inequality and injustice of caste impact our everyday lives; and an intimate and personal glimpse of the ways that human trafficking enslaves and utterly devastates the lives of millions around the world.

This matters greatly to me because it is very, very personal.

One by one, most of my family and friends have become one of the millions counted as those trafficked. They have been lied to, coerced, drugged, kidnapped, transported far away from home, held against their will, and forced to have sex with countless men in brothels that are darker and more dangerous than you dare imagine.

This book tells my story and the stories of my sisters … two are my biological sisters, and two are friends who are as dear to me as a sister. Each one has experienced such unbelievable hardship and misfortune that, at times, it will seem impossible to be true. You might think, *Can this be factual? Is this made up or sensationalized?*

But each word of this story *is* true.

This is not a movie; this is a real-life story.

Each of my sisters was trafficked to India's brothels from Nepal when they were very young, and each one escaped or was rescued. You may not know this, but this is miraculous. Unusual. Extraordinary. Not many girls ever make it out and live to tell of their experience in the brothels. Even fewer live free and live with the healing and hope that I see alive and well in the bodies, minds, and spirits of my sisters.

For the few who have become free, it is rare to talk about what happened because it is difficult—at times, excruciating—to speak of their trauma. It took extraordinary courage for my sisters to raise their voices and proclaim what is true for the world to hear, thus becoming targets for shame or judgment by others, or for retaliation by brutal brothel owners or traffickers.

Yes, my sisters are more than survivors. They are heroes.

I believe that you, too, will be deeply moved and inspired by them.

And yet, to suggest that my sisters are *deeply moving* and *inspiring heroes* is preposterous to many. You see, each one of us is a "low-caste" woman.

Unimportant. Disposable. Worthless.

I am from a community—or "caste"—in Nepal called *Badi*. (You'll learn much more about all of this in the pages to come.) My people—the *Badi*—are called *the untouchables of the untouchables* and *the dust of Nepal*. Still today, we are denied citizenship, unable to own land, go to school, worship, eat, sit near those who are of a higher caste … simply because we are *Badi*.

Many in Nepal would scoff at the idea of us as inspiring or heroic, likely saying something to one another like, "This is outrageous! Who would ever want to read a book about *them?*" At times, I agree with them. I feel like I'm dreaming. *A book about us? This is crazy, unimaginable!*

Why, you might ask? Well, my friend, once again, I say: you'll have to read the book to understand this fully.

Even though I feel like I'm dreaming sometimes, I *have* dreamed for years that our story would be written. In fact, there were times when I earnestly looked and prayed for someone to write my story just as I told it: fully true *and* in a way that would move the hearts of many.

When I met Sarah Davison-Tracy, stayed in her home, and met her family and community, I came to see that she was the one to craft our story. It was a long wait, but we found the right person to write this book. I know it, with all my heart.

I talk with people all the time, not just about this book but about the deep friendship and trust that Sarah and I share. Of course, briefly, much is different between us: I am Nepali, and she is American. My first language is Nepali, and hers is English. Overall, the food we eat, the clothes we wear, and many of our experiences are very, very different.

And yet, we are connected ... and committed.

We understand each other, deeply.

We love each other, very much.

Although I sometimes have felt embarrassed and wish my English were better, Sarah has been able to make sense of our story and my translation of my sisters' stories into English. Whatever my sisters and I have said, she somehow understands and has helped us communicate what we've never spoken to anyone, ever, for the world to read.

When Sarah and I first began talking about how best to craft this book, I knew I wanted to invite several of my sisters to join us.

So, that's just what I did. I asked them.

My story is incomplete without theirs—and theirs without mine.

At first, my sisters didn't see it that way. At times, I felt like I had to work very hard to convince them to speak up. I had to make a strong case for why they should consider this idea that seemed to them utterly crazy, terrifying, impossible.

I understood their hesitancy and fear because they have been through a lot in their lives. I saw why it was that they *never* wanted to share their whole story with *anyone*. It seemed too difficult. It would be traumatic. They wanted to keep the past in the past and try to build a new life.

I understood ... and yet, I didn't back down. I didn't back down because I believed that this story would not just help others, but it would also help them to heal, be empowered, and be connected to me, to Sarah, to the world.

I told my sisters my story—every single part of it. I held nothing back from them. Even though I was never trafficked, they came to see how much I suffered, how many people tried to abuse me, and how I had been lied to. My heart was broken, and trust was broken, repeatedly. I shared with them my passion to use that pain to share hope and freedom with others.

We talked about how our stories could elevate the value of girls and women—especially those who are most vulnerable and marginalized. It was this hope that got them first curious and open and, eventually, proud and excited to join this storytelling project.

We have put our hearts into this book. We have risked a lot—our safety and security, and what people in our community may think about us—so that people will be inspired and believe that every life matters, including those forgotten, invisible, or dismissed like so many *Badi* girls.

One day, we are going to die, but this book will live on.

I have *so many hopes and dreams* for this book.

I want people around the world to read and be changed by this history-making story.

I want it to change the mindset of our government. Our message is for our government. Maybe one day soon, they will say, "They are standing, fighting for their rights. They are human beings and deserve freedom and opportunity."

My legal and professionally known name is "Devisara Badi," but I am known by many in my family, community, and friends around the world as "Hannah." In this book, I call myself "Hannah."

I have a big dream that I want to share with you and put into print this very day. I want to become the prime minister of Nepal. "Impossible!" some might say. "A *Badi* girl as prime minister? Never!" But there is a saying, "Impossible things are possible in God's hands!" And remember, many said that this book was impossible too.

I believe that our stories—yours and mine—will become connected in these pages. My friend, I pray for you—really, I do—for your hopes and dreams to come true.

I hope, with all my heart, that you come to love and care for my sisters as I do and that you one day join me in my fight against human trafficking. When you are ready, reach out to me. I will be there, with open arms, to welcome you to the fight. Because make no mistake: I will keep fighting. My sisters, my people, every person around the world are worth it.

Here's to impossible dreams and making history, together.

–**Devisara "Hannah" Badi,**
CEO of Himalayan Entrepreneur Resources (HER),
an empowerment initiative in Nepal that gives health, safety,
and autonomy to marginalized women so they can live free
from sexual exploitation and abuse

First picture ever taken of me | 2008

My village | 2021

Badi children and me | 2021

Distributing health kits to Badi women | 2020

A photo of me: Devisara "Hannah" Badi | 2020

Contents

Geography

Cities / Villages / Districts Referenced

- Nepal
  - Kathmandu
  - *Badi* Villages: Nayagau, Jhuprakhola, Chinchu, Ramghat, Mehelkuna
  - Nepalgunj
  - Surkhet (city and district)
  - Bardiya (city and district)
- India
  - New Delhi: G.B. Road (Garstin Bastion Road), Ghazipur ("Trash Mountain"), Meerut
  - Rupaidiha

Hannah's Family Tree

Villagers in Nepal
Chaha—sold Meena, Puja, Gita
Garvesh—sold Aasha
Ram—sold Meena
Ditya—ma'am whose house Hannah broke into to find Jiya
Prayan—Ditya's son / proposed to Jiya

Nepali Support Team
Raju—founder and president of Lighthouse Foundation Nepal
Håkan—founder of Out of Ashes, collaborator / friend of Raju's
Sangeeta—caretaker and PTSD counselor
Mr. and Mrs. Janak—rescued Khushi
Bahadur—helped in the rescue of Meena's daughters

People in India
Munna—moved Kushi into new brothel
Rajesh—customer who fell in love with Meena / helped in Meena's and Rahul's rescue

Family
Maya—Hannah, Meena, Aasha's mom
Bir—Hannah, Meena, Aasha's dad
*Meena—Hannah's eldest sister
*Aasha—Hannah's older sister
Bishal—Aasha's husband
Meena's children—Anas, Bina, Kaya, Nanu, Rahul
Aasha's children—Preeti, Suraj

Friends
*Sakhira—friend of Hannah's
Mahesh—Sakhira's husband
*Khushi—friend of Hannah's
Jiya—friend of Hannah's
Gita—one of Hannah's friends
Puja—one of Hannah's friends

One of our 5 storytellers

Prologue

The rickshaw motor hums and whirs as we careen through the dark night. Hands gripping the wheel and eyes alert, the driver seems single-minded in his determination to deliver his cargo on time. A hearty bundle of Indian *rupees* awaits him if he does.

The streets around us are filled with the sounds of beer bottles clanging, food sizzling, and *Bollywood* music blaring. Men are everywhere: walking, eating—and looking.

There is a lot to look at around here. Some girls hang out of windows from above, tempting the many men on the street below to come closer. Others stand in doorways, their lips painted bright red, swaying their hips seductively. I see a man in one of the brothel doorways—I know him to be a pimp. He urges passing men to stop. "You want a *keti* (girl)? You are in the right place! We have many young and beautiful girls for you here … I give you a good price!"

Some men leer from afar, and others line up, waiting their turn to enter the brothel's rooms above. Others seem not to pay much attention to the scene surrounding them as they sit in clusters and spit dark red *paan* on the ground.

This is Garstin Bastion Road—known as G.B. Road—in the city of New Delhi. It is one of India's most well-known red-light districts.

I shudder at how well I know this place—and its foul stink of sex. At nine years old, I was abducted from my village in Nepal and trafficked to India as a sex slave and house servant to three brothers.

India has been a dangerous place for me ever since. But right now, it is particularly perilous. I wonder, *Do my captors know about my plan to leave the city tonight?* If so, I'm sure they're already scouring the streets on bikes, on foot, and in rickshaws—desperate to capture me, their "property." If they do, the brothel *bosses* will be very, very angry, and I will be badly beaten—or worse. I have belonged to them for thirteen years and have no right to do what I am trying to do today: escape.

We're getting close to the meeting point where Rajesh and my *aama* (mom) await. If all goes well, I will soon see my four children in Kathmandu. One by one, each was rescued and has been protected from becoming one of the thousands of women and children enslaved in G.B. Road's brothels.

I tell myself to stay focused on getting out of this city. I take a deep breath, tighten my jaw, and scan the crowds for anyone I recognize from the brothel.

In ten minutes, my rickshaw rounds a corner, and I see him, waiting right where he promised. Rajesh's eyes light up and, wasting no time, he makes his way to the rickshaw, pays the driver, and directs me into a waiting taxi, where I find my *aama*. As I collapse into the seat, my mother wraps her arms tightly around me and whispers tearful prayers of gratitude that I made it safely. Closing my eyes, I rest my head on her shoulder as the car speeds toward the border of India and Nepal.

After thirteen long years as a sex slave in the brothels of New Delhi, during which I estimate I "serviced" twenty thousand men, this is the day of my rescue and return home to Nepal.

Beginnings—
Context and Understanding

Sarah: The Bridge-Builder

A Surprising Request (2015)

Three months before this woman fled for her life through the streets of New Delhi, I heard her name for the first time in my home, halfway around the world in the United States. Over steaming cups of *chai*, Hannah, a young woman from Nepal, told me the story of her *didi* (elder sister), Meena. Hannah hoped for the day Meena would be safely home in Nepal and reunited with her four children. She worried that her sister was dying—Meena was bleeding profusely after being abused by thousands upon thousands of men for more than a decade. Tears rolled down her cheeks and mine, the pile of tissues growing as we conversed about the fate of Hannah's sister.

A few weeks before Hannah and I met, my family and friends excitedly prepared for our guests to arrive from Nepal. Our home was full of gifts and welcome notes—all ready and waiting for their arrival. We'd heard that they loved bike riding, so our garage looked like a bike shop, thanks to generous friends and neighbors. There were a dozen bikes ready to be ridden, lined up side by side with helmets resting on their handlebars.

One friend donated water bottles for each guest provided by an organization that works with women in Kenya. Another creative friend crafted handmade bags, with each name written in a calligraphic script. We hoped that our guests would feel welcome and know that they had a place with us in our home and our community.

Finally, the day of their arrival came, and our Nepali guests began to stream through our front door. In a blink, our house was jam-packed and noisily energetic. We showed them to their rooms, where our bedroom floors were covered wall-to-wall with air mattresses. Before they fell asleep that night—and each night during their visit—*Bollywood* tunes (music from Indian movies) crept out from under their doorways, accented by the sounds of whispers and laughter. Meal after meal each day was a celebration, an extravaganza of flavors and stories, which inevitably turned into a boisterous and lively dance party.

Our visitors were part of an international nonprofit committed to advocating for children who are at risk of becoming victims of human trafficking. Their team of six included three leaders of the organization and three young women whose lives had been transformed—and truthfully, saved—by the work of this organization.

The group's aim for their tour through the United States was to bring awareness to the world about the human rights abuses happening among a marginalized community in Nepal called the *Badi*. They intended to connect with people through the power of their stories, build lifelong relationships, and raise funds for the work yet to be done.

Knowing how I love to create community, whether as a family or through the global organization I founded, a friend had asked if I would be willing to host the Nepalis on their tour stop in Colorado. We created a series of community events that took place via online video calls and in-person gatherings, in living rooms and backyards, at universities and restaurants, in the mountains and in downtown Denver. Our Colorado community came in droves, spilling into overflow spaces and staying until late into the evening, in awe of the stories and unbelievable resilience of our new friends.

We held our breath as our visitors told their unbelievable accounts of little girls and long-enslaved women being protected and rescued and escaping from brothels. We were in awe of their inner strength and faith that fueled their fight for justice. They shared their stories and spoke about the complex issues of caste, poverty, marginalization, and human trafficking. It wasn't easy to hear, and people responded differently—some were overwhelmed and shocked, others incensed and awakened. Many were eager to do what they could to join them in their efforts.

My calling to join them came unexpectedly—as most callings do—on a stunner of a day in Denver. I was driving our guests to a speaking event. We had the windows down, and as usual, music blared from the radio. As our car turned into a *Bollywood* dance party and the young women sang at the top of their lungs, I was about to have a conversation that would change my life. I remember right where we were—at a stoplight at one of the major intersections in our city. To our right was a gas station, and to our left was a strip club with their latest weekly message posted for all to read: "Toxic masculinity welcome here."

Lost in momentary thought, I contemplated the words of this sign alongside the stories of my friends. I was struck by the parallels between this strip club in my American city and the ways these young Nepali women's lives had been catastrophically impacted by the business of selling sex. My jaw tightened, and I gripped the steering wheel in anger as I considered the ways in which this global reality is both toxic *and* dangerous for so many, including very young children.

"Sarah *didi*! I have the best idea, sister!" My new friend Raju drew me away from my momentary ire. "It's you! You are going to write our story. Yes, you're the one!"

The dancing and singing in the car suddenly stopped, and it grew quiet. The whole car seemed to be listening to his words—part declaration and part invitation.

"We have been talking and dreaming for nearly five years about writing a book that will tell the story of what has been happening in Nepal among the *Badi* people. We have been waiting to find the right person to write this story. It's *you!* I have no doubt!"

I had goosebumps. I felt it, sensing that this might be one of those moments that would change my destiny and set me on a new path.

I was silent as Raju spoke. He shared how much it had impacted their team to feel so welcome at home with our family and showered with love by our community. He grew a bit quieter and yet was deeply thunderous in my heart as he shared, "Although there are differences between us, we feel like you are one of us." I looked in the rearview mirror and saw my young friends smiling and nodding. To be sure, I'd felt it too: something extraordinary was going on among us.

Raju continued, "We have felt such ease here. This is not natural for us, especially for the three girls. Someday, you will learn why this is so significant, Sarah *didi*. They have been excluded and wronged for much of their lives by so many. But here, and with you, they feel good, and they are happy. They trust you." His voice cracked with emotion, and he asked, "So, *didi*, what do you say? Will you do it?"

I had little conception of the details of timing or how it would work, but my heart raced. Although everything in me wanted to shout an immediate "Yes!" I knew I needed to take some time for reflection and discernment. I took a breath, looked at my friends, and responded, "Thank you for this honor and invitation. I will think and pray about it." As I did, it didn't take long to sense that my answer was indeed yes.

Soon it was time for them to head off to their next tour stop. Although we were excited for the book's development in the future, it was a tearful farewell for everyone. Within ten days' time, a most extraordinary and deep bond had formed between us. As the girls and I embraced, they shared their love and gratitude and their hopes that we would meet again. I tearfully whispered to each one, "I love you, too, *bahini* (little sister)."

Five months later, I went to Nepal to be with my friends and begin the process of writing their stories. When they took me to the far west of Nepal to their *Badi* villages, our connection and commitment to work together grew even stronger. As we made our way on the twenty-hour drive, singing loudly to *Bollywood* music and nodding off for naps, I asked questions and they told stories. We feasted at roadside open-air restaurants and in homes. For a few long stretches of empty road, I hopped behind the wheel and drove through deeply forested paved roads.

In their villages, we listened to *Badi* community leaders speak of what was most needed and to parents lamenting sick or missing children. A few evenings, our feet pounded the dirt as we danced together until late in the night. Two families begged us to take their teenage daughters back with us to school and to the safe house dormitories in Kathmandu. They worried that if the girls stayed much longer in the village, they would disappear like so many others. Just like that, our five-passenger car had six passengers squeezed in like sardines.

We spent one afternoon with a bundle of beautiful children who were playing outside their home as their mothers got ready for a night of *work* across the street at a *Badi* village brothel. I understood as we sat together, sharing snacks and smiling for selfies, that without intervention, these beauties faced a perilous future.

I returned home resolute to craft this story with my Nepali friends. Over the next year and a half, I reached out a few times and asked if they were ready to begin the book. "No, *didi*. Not yet, sister." A few months later, when they were ready, they reached out, saying, "We are ready!" At that time, I had begun to write another book and knew the timing wasn't quite right. But at the end of 2017, the answer was an enthusiastic "*Hunchha!*" (Yes!) for all of us.

It was time to begin.

Hannah, our lead storyteller, quickly went to work inviting and gathering the others. One by one, they told their stories—many spoken for the very first time—and Hannah translated. *No Longer Untouchable* began to take shape in what we hoped would become the first *kitab* (book) published in English about the *Badi*.

I was captivated by their courage and in awe of their resilience in the face of experiences of violence and pain that I could barely wrap my head around. Their stories and voices seized my imagination. They just didn't give up. I was inspired and determined to do the same.

As we sent out advanced reader copies of the book, endorsements began to flood in from around the world. Our US publishing team worked tirelessly. The cover design, interior book layout, and all the minutia of publishing a book were happening right on schedule. In March 2019, it was nearly finished. We made plans for it to be published in the summer.

But it was not to be.

Quite suddenly, the swift publishing pace slowed, suddenly shifting to an almost indistinguishable pace of, say, a slow turtle.

The storytellers' voices grew quiet and ultimately silent.

I worried. *What is going on? Are my friends okay? Will this book ever see the light of day?* Some days, I wondered if there had been a misunderstanding or unintended hurt, despite our years of friendship and commitment to be open and honest.

Amid the flurry of thoughts and moments of worry, I sensed it clearly in my heart: *Wait. Trust. Do not jump to any conclusions of what this means or what's going on with your friends until you know it to be true, directly from them. Believe the best. Surrender. The timing is not what you expected, but this process cannot be forced or controlled by you.*

I prayed for my sisters' safety and well-being, for their protection, for their futures. I prayed for the book to be birthed into the world at just the right time.

One week of silence turned into two, then stretched to a month, and then longer still. The summer publishing dream date was not to be. Nor was the fall or winter. I had lots of time to practice waiting, trusting, surrendering, believing, and praying. The year 2020 came and almost went with very little word. I sent periodic texts to check in, but for the most part, I heard little for more than a year and a half.

What I did hear from my friends was that life had grown complicated and challenging for each of our storytellers in Nepal. A few grew afraid to share their story. They feared that even though all names but Hannah's were changed, others would figure out who they were. It was scary. They felt ashamed. What would their families, friends, or their current or future husbands think?

Telling a story like this takes courage. It takes a community of support and love. It takes trust—loads of it—to give voice to intimate and painful stories like these. It takes tenacity and vision and a *why* that is big enough to overcome the fear and naysayers.

Just weeks before the end of the ever-tumultuous year of 2020, I received word from Hannah. They were ready and excited to finish what we started.

Their *whys* had overcome their fear and strengthened their dedication to publish this book. Their voices began rising, once again, and their determination was more resolute than ever. One sister said, "We want to share our stories about being trafficked so that others are spared from what we experienced." Another added, "With faith, family, and friends, we believe it is possible to heal and to rise up, even from the ashes of life in a brothel. We want to share that hope is never dead … is never over." And a third joined the others, "Even though we feel afraid, at times, we know it is important to share these stories about our experience, our country, and our *Badi* people."

And so, we picked up right where we had left off and finished the book.

Which brings us to this moment.

Welcome.

We are honored and deeply grateful that you are here.

Caste and the Badi People

Central to this story and our five storytellers, whom you will soon meet, is the reality of caste—social stratification—in Nepal. Caste discrimination affects an estimated 260 million people worldwide, the vast majority of whom live in South Asia. It is considered by many to be one of the strongest racist phenomena in the world.

During the Malla dynasty (1201–1779), the caste system was introduced into Nepal. While it was officially abolished and made illegal to discriminate based on caste in 1962, our storytellers have experienced countless ways in which this system is still practiced today.

This hierarchy has been strongly embedded into the culture, and it dictates the way people relate to one another in everyday life. In the caste system, a person's last name announces their caste and their expected profession, delineating one's social and economic standing, work, marriage prospects, opportunities for education, and more.

Within the caste system, the *Dalits* or *untouchables* are believed to be inherently impure, such that it is unacceptable to be in close physical proximity with them. Touching anything they may have touched or walking on a path where they may have walked is believed to contaminate or pollute someone of a higher caste.

Among the *Dalits*, there are levels of hierarchy as well. Sometimes called *the dust of Nepal* or *the untouchables of the untouchables*, the lowest of all among the *Dalits* are the *Badi*. For hundreds of years, the *Badi* made their living as entertainers, performing songs and dances and telling stories at festivals, weddings, and private parties. *Badi* translates to "musical people," and they were often sought-after musicians, singers, and dancers.

In the 1950s, several events occurred that impacted the livelihoods of the *Badi* and catapulted them into extreme poverty that has continued to this day. In 1951, the Rana oligarchy ended in Nepal, which created a cascading ripple effect that shifted power structures and reduced opportunities for work among the *Badi* and other low-caste communities. Two other significant factors entered the mix in the 1960s: the population increased in the far west of Nepal, where the *Badi* were located, and access to radio and television for entertainment expanded. As jobs became harder to come by and the *Badi* were less frequently employed for entertainment, poverty expanded and deepened. To compensate for their significant loss in employment, *Badi* women began to more frequently and openly turn to prostitution for their livelihood.

The *Badi* have had little to no access to education, healthcare, land ownership, and citizenship. Most *Badi* are illiterate. Teachers and higher-caste children have frequently banned *Badi* and other low-caste *Dalit* children from their classrooms. Until this generation, no known *Badi* children ever progressed beyond the sixth grade.

One-third of *Badi* are homeless, and two-thirds are living on public or government land. Nearly 75 percent of *Badi* men migrate to search for employment. In Nepal, the births of children with unknown fathers have often not been registered. In 2005, the Nepal Supreme Court declared that Badi children were entitled to registration and citizenship, although many *Badi* do not have birth certificates or evidence of citizenship, which impacts their access to school, jobs, and voting rights.

These complex and far-reaching factors have created the devastating reality that prostitution and selling girls to traffickers have become sources of income for many *Badi* families. Even while a woman is pregnant, it is common for her to be approached by a trafficker, who offers her a deposit in exchange for the promise that if she gives birth to a girl, that girl will be sold to the trafficker. Generally, when the girl is around ten years old, the trafficker will return for the girl, pay the family, and take her to a brothel where she is enslaved as a sex *worker*—mostly likely, for the rest of her life.

The *Badi* are perfect human trafficking targets: vulnerable, desperate, and, according to many, the worthless *dust of Nepal*.

Human Trafficking

Human trafficking is a heartbreaking—and potentially overwhelming—reality that has impacted each of our storytellers, their families, and their communities. While the numbers and statistics may seem nearly impossible to grasp, they are included to give you a sense of its massive scope and to make a case for why it is so critically important that people worldwide do more to counter this immense injustice.

Globally, the statistics for the total number of people trafficked vary greatly—by millions. The most frequent source cited by international human rights organizations is the International Labour Organization (ILO), which reported that in 2016, 40.3 million people were victims of modern slavery and that one in four of those victims were children. Furthermore, the ILO documents that in 2016, 4.8 million people were in forced sexual exploitation, and of that number, 99 percent were women. They estimate that human trafficking generates about $150 billion a year in revenue. Human trafficking ranks third in organized crime, after the sale of arms and drugs.

In Nepal, it is estimated that 15,000 women and 5,000 girls each year are trafficked out of the country for the purpose of sexual exploitation and profit. Many are trafficked before they reach ten years old since virgins and young girls are more profitable. Once sold, a girl is forced to stay until her purchase price, often called her "debt," is paid back. It is a nearly impossible task, and most never repay their debt or leave the brothel.

Four of our storytellers were trafficked—lied to, coerced, drugged, kidnapped, and sold to brothels. They are four who escaped, but many millions remain enslaved today.

Although this is the story of five young women and some of their friends and family from Nepal, there are very few places in the world where this human rights atrocity hasn't yet reached. In America and Europe, throughout middle-class neighborhoods with white picket fences, in rich high schools, and among sleepy little towns that look idyllic and safe, sex trafficking pervades. No one is immune from this reality. No place is exempt from sex trafficking's tyranny.

Find Your Story in Theirs

This is not a book that promises to cover the issues or all the systemic causes of human trafficking, caste, or Nepali culture. No, our bigger intention is much simpler—and more intimate—than that. By the time you read the last page of this story, we hope these five brave *bahiniharu* (little sisters) will no longer seem like strangers to you but will become those with whom you feel a bond of connection, changing your life in profound ways.

These women have a knack for transforming lives. They have already begun to alter the narrative of what many believe is possible for their people. They are changemakers who are rewriting history in their country and around the world. They are the first of a handful of *Badi* youth—and other *Dalits*—to have access to education, to own land, and to hold passports. Two of our storytellers were the first known *Badi* girls to travel to America, Europe, and Asia. Their stories are drawing the attention of many, including those in political power in Nepal and filmmakers around the globe.

These firsts are momentous because for much of their lives, they have lived as the outcasts, the nobodies, and the *untouchables*. Their choice to openly share the whole of their stories as *Badi* women is making waves—angering some and inspiring others. To be sure, it is brave and revolutionary.

Depending on where you find yourself today, we have varying intentions for the ways these stories will connect with your own.

To those of you at the end of your rope or discouraged, we hope that as you read, you experience your own resilience, strength, and significance. Purpose often grows out of pain. Not just for our storytellers, but for you. May their experiences beckon you to carry on, to never go it alone, to remember that your story is never *ever* over, and that the very worst can always be transformed into something beautiful.

To those of you open and eager to make a difference in the world, we hope that you respond to the global realities of injustice that beckon and that, as you do, you connect to a community of others. We want to bring awareness that leads to wholehearted action in your everyday life, and we believe this will fuel a movement of many who are unstoppably committed to the well-being of all.

To those who are impassioned and committed leaders in communities, businesses, organizations, and governments around the world, we hope that you expand your influence and become even greater catalysts for justice than ever before. We want these stories to bring needed change in communities and governments around the world so that people are protected and laws are upheld. When this happens, separate silos of *some* will become a collective and unified movement of *many* that will be able to make the critical changes needed globally.

Our world is vast, composed of 7.5 billion people. It is the power of each one of us working together that makes a difference. We've seen it proven true throughout history: people can work together to bring benefit or destruction to the world. The world is changed for the better as we connect and commit to make a difference together.

We believe that while our *whys* may look diverse, each *why* at its root is about making life better for others. Put simply, it is to find ways to be of service to those around us. Whether directly related to human trafficking or mobilizing you to commit to a different arena that is beckoning you, we hope that this book propels you further into your unique *why*.

Consider reading *No Longer Untouchable* as a declaration that you will do your part to make a difference and are willing to be transformed by what you learn. As you read, ponder these questions, "What changes might this story make in my life?" and "What difference am I being invited to make?"

And yet, within the promise and potential of making a difference, reading these stories can be hard. They speak of a world darker than most of us can conceive, in which murder and suicide are everyday occurrences, little girls are locked behind bars and forced to have sex with one man after the next, violence and terror are used to weaken and silence those already traumatized, and those no longer able to be profitable are left on the streets to die. What these young women have lived through is horrifying. Their lives are full of one bad break after another.

These stories will likely pain your heart at times, and you may be tempted to close the book. Tend to yourself as you read.

Take a break, if necessary.

And then come back.

Return to these stories because in them, you will find heroic accounts that will take your breath away and evidence of ways in which the human spirit is unbelievably resilient.

Hope *does* triumph. Love *does* heal. Heroes *do* rise from the dust.

"100 Percent True (Satya)"

We often thought about you—our reader—and wondered if we needed to change these stories slightly, softening them a bit and making them less "hard." In the end, the answer we came to was a resounding "no." The stories that follow have neither been embellished nor made more palatable. Our storytellers expressed a desire for this book to be "100 percent true," and as such, there is nothing fictional or sensationalized within these pages. This story is true. *Satya*.

Truth be told, there are, unfortunately, countless examples around the world of ways in which peoples' stories have been used to manipulate the feelings of the public, all too often with the intent to open the wallets of donors more widely. In fact, one of our storytellers felt the toxic sting of this reality when she was asked by a major supporter to tweak the truth to make her story "more compelling" for greater interest and funding.

The team of storytellers in Nepal and I have spent countless hours poring over interview notes and have sent hundreds of emails back and forth between Nepal and the United States. These stories have been told, read, and approved by each storyteller. We worked with a Nepali consultant to do whatever is in our power to ensure that these stories are accurate and true.

Each young woman—except for Hannah—was rescued or escaped from being held captive in brothels. Their former captors are not happy that these women are no longer their property. In telling their stories, these storytellers risk their lives. Thus, at their request, all their names—except for Hannah's—have been changed to protect their identities and security. If the names get confusing, kindly refer to the "family tree" at the beginning and the references section at the back of the book.

Also, please note that throughout these stories, we have used a few words from the Nepali language. We have done so to give those who don't speak Nepali a glimpse and experience of the language of our storytellers. Most often, we have included the English translation in parentheses or have referenced the meaning of the word directly after its use. For your convenience, there is also a glossary of Nepali and Hindi words in the references section of the book.

And now, it is time to introduce you to our extraordinary storytellers.

In Their Own Words

Hannah (Part One): The Warrior

The Roots of Prostitution

The whirling dancing of our *Badi* women *is* beautiful. The mysterious music of our people *does* captivate. Art *is* in our blood and in our DNA; it is what we *do* and who we *are*. We are *Badi*, the *musical people*.

Prostitution started three hundred years ago among the *Badi*, during a time when many in our community were poor. At that time, our women were masterful performers, chosen by one king after the next to dance at their palaces. In a complex mix of poverty, caste, power, and lust, sex became linked to the expectations of *Badi* women's entertainment.

Politics in our country are complicated; the pendulum of power has swayed between the royalty, the religious, and the democratic. For hundreds of years, when kings were pleased with a group of *Badi* people, they gave them land. When the Rana regime was overthrown in 1950, the government sought to take away the power of the royalty and wealthy throughout the country; they also began to take back the land from the *Badi*.

Within a generation, the only place for many *Badi* communities to live was on land undesirable to others. Our villages began to crop up next to polluted highways, flood-plain riverbeds, and in insect-ridden jungles. Education, jobs, security, and respect from others—all already tenuous at best—rapidly fell away.

The rich and powerful no longer had money to hire our women. We were not ever wealthy; struggle has been a part of *Badi* life. But we became an even poorer people. We became an even hungrier people.

We plummeted from the palaces into poverty, from being admired to being considered abhorrent, from being celebrated to being sold.

A Recycled Story

People in power created the caste system, this hierarchical way of treating people. Your name declares your caste. Your caste determines your value. It is a system of oppression created by humans.

Generally, we *Dalits* are hard workers. We have had to be to survive. Historically, we've been given the jobs that no one else wanted to do. It's ironic and maddening that the *Dalits* have built most of the statues and temples in Nepal, but we are not permitted to touch those statues or enter the temples we built. We make most of the pots used for cooking in Nepal, but we cannot go inside the home of a higher-caste person where those pots are being used. It is believed that we make unclean whatever we touch. Many call us *untouchable*.

Countless *Badi* children have high-caste fathers. These high-caste men come to our village the most … and the most often. What is absurd is that we are not allowed to walk on the same path as those of higher castes, or to sit in the same places as they sit, but when it comes to sex, not only are we no longer *untouchable*, but they *demand entry* into our bodies.

We have been mistreated and crushed by discrimination, poverty, and sexual exploitation for far too long. Among the *Badi*, for many years, it has been believed that women's sole purpose is to satisfy the sexual cravings of men. Whether wealthy or poor, men have treated us as though we are alive purely for their sexual pleasure.

When I was born in 1995, sexual exploitation and trafficking had become the fate and the way of life for most *Badi* women. When I was growing up, men would climb through the windows of our village homes, offering to pay our fathers a dollar or even a glass of *rakshi* (homemade liquor) for sex with their daughters.

Many among our people have come to see girls as property, as lucrative assets, to be bought and sold. Selling their women to traffickers became one of the ways families generated funds to survive—at least, that's what they told themselves. Over and over, husbands sold their wives, mothers sold their unborn babies, and family members kidnapped and took their own to brothels in distant cities. Until now, *Badi* girls have had little to no choice. None. We have been told what to do and where to go for generations.

As a girl, I remember looking around the village and seeing so many things that were wrong. Girls were disappearing and being trafficked; husbands regularly beat and mistreated their wives. It seemed to me that women did most of the work, and most men did little to nothing all day long except get drunk and play games in the shade of jungle trees or under the covered porches of our village huts. Our women worked from pre-dawn until late at night, gathering firewood, sometimes farming bits of vacant land, collecting stones and slate from the river to sell to merchants, cooking the little food we had, and raising children.

Today, my *buba* (dad) is a very good and kind man. But in years past, he wasn't. I have heard the hard stories about him from my sisters and *aama*. He used to beat my mom and have affairs, bring girls home and force my mom to watch them have sex.

My parents often slept outside to make room for my siblings and me to sleep inside our hut. Shelter in our village didn't provide much protection from the blistering heat in the summer or torrential rain during monsoons. In the winter, we had no blankets for warmth, and even though my sisters and I would sleep close to each other for warmth, we shivered all night long and only slept a little. Our skin was perpetually covered with itchy bug bites.

I ran around without clothes most of the time. Perhaps that's why the day my dad handed me a gift is etched forever in my memory. I was seven. He'd gone to India for work—as do many *Badi* people—and brought back a t-shirt he'd bought for me in a market. It was the first new shirt I'd ever owned. I remember running my fingers over the soft cotton. I loved its new smell and wore it with pride until it turned to tatters.

I do not recall very many occasions of lightheartedness or laughter as a child, but the moments of playfulness inevitably involved my best friends, Gita and Puja. On hot afternoons in the summer, we swam in the river, splashing in its refreshing, cool waters. Sometimes, one of my big sisters would pull out the *madal* (a Nepali drum), and we would dance, spinning to the music and singing our favorite *Badi* songs at the top of our lungs. But those moments were few and far between. Life was full of more hardship than levity for my friends and me.

When my two best friends and sister went missing, I was eight years old. Gita and Puja disappeared first, then my sister Aasha. My big sister, Meena, had disappeared the year before. It was far too common for our *Badi* girls to vanish, but the disappearance of these four undid me. I was tied up in knots of worry, with no idea where they were. Finally, we received word that Gita and Puja had been trafficked to a brothel in India by Chaha—a brothel owner, pimp, and their cousin. It would take years to find out where Aasha and Meena were taken and whether they were alive.

I was split between two emotions: heaving with sorrow at one moment and feeling like I would explode with anger the next. I might have been an uneducated and *untouchable Badi* girl, but I knew that this way of life was not right. I knew it was unjust for a family member to abduct and sell her very own cousin to a brothel far from home. I was vexed with unanswerable questions: *Are my friends and sisters okay, alive, or dead? Is there something I can do to bring them home?* Ultimately, I was heartbroken and felt powerless to change the way my people were treated by others, as well as the way they treated each other.

I clearly saw that as the oppression from outside increased, it also increased from my own community members. Even though others called us *the dust of Nepal,* we ourselves pounded each other into smaller fragments of dust. I believed it was a recycled story: For generations, we were mistreated and shackled by others. Now, we were doing the same—or worse—to our own.

Part-Time Child Soldier (2003)

In 1996, a political party called the Nepal Communist Party—also known as the *Maoists*—began using our village in western Nepal as a base for their military operations. According to the *Encyclopedia Britannica,* their aim was to overthrow Nepal's monarchy and replace it with a democratically elected government. They launched a guerrilla war, which lasted ten years and resulted in the deaths of more than twelve thousand Nepalis. Human rights groups criticized them for their alleged use of underage soldiers. Finally, in 2006, the United Nations brokered a peace treaty, and the war ended.

I was just one year old when the Maoists first came to our village. Over the next ten years, they came and went, sometimes staying for months at a time. Our village became a war zone as the Maoists and police battled each other. Day after day, our huts trembled with gunfire and bullets ricocheted around us.

As I grew older, I was sometimes forced to help the police, and at other times, the Maoists. They *told* us what to do—we were never asked. We were being used to fight a war that wasn't ours. It wasn't right. No, not at all. Our people's powerlessness filled me with anger.

When I was eight years old, I remember one Maoist soldier who walked through our village each morning and methodically counted how many men, women, and children were in each home. On many occasions, he would return with more soldiers late at night and bring enormous, terrifying dogs with them. The dogs barked wildly as the men banged on our doors to wake us up, shouting: "Women, men, and children—all of you, meet us outside immediately!"

We did as they demanded and stood outside as the soldiers scanned the crowd. Some nights, if they had heavy gear to carry, they chose our strongest men to help them in their mission. On other nights, they selected my sisters, friends, and me. Tucking bombs and grenades into our small and nimble hands, they needed our knowledge of the jungle to transport weapons safely and secretly through the moonlit terrain.

I remember hearing parents tearfully whisper their worries to one another as we walked away. *Will they come back? Where are they taking our* bachchaharu (children) *this time?* We would hear stories from nearby villages of children who never returned from their mission because they'd died—perhaps tripping while carrying their bombs or because they were made to join the Maoist forces as a full-time child soldier. Lucky for us, my friends and I always came back. Yet, these were dark, difficult, and violent days.

After the firefights, dead bodies were everywhere. My friends and I would pick through the pockets and backpacks of the soldiers and police officers lying on the ground, in search of food and money ... anything of value.

I remember coming across the body of a dead soldier one morning. He was wearing boots that looked brand new. I was ecstatic as I took them off, ran home, and proudly presented them to my *buba*. My dad's eyes twinkled as he looked at me and held those boots, murmuring with surprise, "These are so special, *chhori* (daughter)!" He'd never owned anything new. He wore them proudly for five years until his toes finally wore through and poked out of the leather.

One morning, after a fierce battle the night before, hundreds of lifeless bodies were scattered throughout our village and on the riverbed. My friends and I were busy for days, shouting with excitement when we found food or other treasures in the backpacks and pockets of the dead.

Sometimes we collected bomb fragments, grenade casings, and bullet shells and wove the glittering metal pieces together, making necklaces and bracelets that jingled as we walked. Little did I know that these trinkets made from bombshell fragments would soon save the life of my cousin and me.

One afternoon, as my cousin and I attempted to hide outside the school's window to listen to the day's lesson, the teacher and students ran us off the school grounds. Furious, they didn't want us—*untouchable Badi* kids—contaminating them by sitting nearby.

This had happened many times before, but on this day, it made me angrier than ever. Vowing to my cousin to return the next day, I furrowed my brow and declared, "Going to school is my biggest dream. This teacher and high-caste kids are not going to stop me!"

We walked home as I fumed at yet another failed attempt to take a step toward my dream. When my cousin suddenly broke into a run, I shouted, "What are you doing?" As he sprinted, he yelled back that he saw a ball in the road ahead.

Watching him sprint, I felt fear in my gut. *Something is wrong.* I began chasing after him, and as I approached my cousin and looked at the ball in his hands, I knew right away what it was. The *ball* was made of the same metal my friends and I collected for jewelry after the firefights in our village. I had seen this metal's exploded fragments many times. *This is a bomb.*

I grabbed the bomb-ball from him, intending to hurl it as hard and as far as I could. The bomb practically exploded up and out of my hands and splintered trees in two as it blasted its way through the jungle, blowing a burst of hot air and dust into our faces. My cousin and I looked at each other dazedly through the smoke, and we began to make our way home.

While the bomb's blast echoed and made my ears ring uncomfortably for weeks, I knew my cousin and I would have died if I'd taken even a second or two more to throw the bomb away. We were lucky, and I knew it.

A Dangerous Doctor (2004)

When I say that life was difficult for me and for my family, I mean to say that worrying wrecked me. Within the span of just one year, I was forced to carry weapons for the Maoists, hurled the bomb into the forest, one sister died of typhoid fever, and two sisters disappeared, along with my best friends, Puja and Gita. I was filled with dread that I would be next. Hunger was the daily norm as a child, and my stomach ached for food from the time I woke up until I went to bed. Having little access to healthcare, sickness and death surrounded me, and I watched many in our village die from illness and disease.

Later that year, I became physically sick. My mouth was stuck in a strange sideways position. I had migraine headaches and often blacked out. I had a hard time talking and thinking. Finally, my parents grew so concerned that my *buba* took me to the hospital.

It was not an easy journey. He and I walked partway and took the bus the rest of the way. Walking was slow going, and I had to sit down often to catch my breath. I remember that my dad was patient, but I sensed he was worried by my frequent requests to rest. After a half-day of travel, we finally arrived in Nepalgunj, a sizable city in Nepal near the border of India, and we made our way to the hospital.

After my medical examination, the doctor called my dad in, saying, "Your *chhori* has a buildup of fluid in her brain. Not only that, but she is severely malnourished. Although her health is not good, with better nutrition, medicine, and a few visits back to the hospital, the good news is that your daughter will be okay." He instructed us to return for treatment as soon as we were able.

As we headed home, my dad was silent … and crestfallen. We both knew that our family had no money to pay for my treatment. We got home just before sunset, and word quickly spread through the village about the doctor's diagnoses.

Over the next week, a flood of friends and family knocked on our door, each giving my dad whatever *rupees* (Nepali currency) they could spare. Each gift was an enormous sacrifice. No one had much, and I knew it. Day by day, the pile of *rupees* grew sufficient for me to return to the hospital for treatment and medicine.

My *buba* and I again made our way to the hospital in Nepalgunj. This time, I was in more pain and weaker than before. Barely able to walk, I was given a wheelchair at check-in. Once in an exam room, a doctor walked in and began to review my medical file. When he saw my name, he exclaimed loudly, "Oh, you are *Badi!*"

In that moment, the feeling in the room changed. Even though my dad was in the room, the doctor's eyes leered, and he looked at me in a way that made my skin crawl with discomfort. Anxious, I looked at the floor.

The doctor walked over to me and briskly wheeled me away from my father. We entered an X-ray room, the door clicked shut, and the room was quiet. It was just the doctor and me. He switched off the lights.

I was shaking and uneasy. My mind was whirring with questions. *Why are the lights off? Why didn't he let my dad come with us?* When he told me to take off my clothes for the X-ray, I grew even more nervous. *Something isn't right. Not right at all. What to do?* Once again, I felt I had no choice other than to do as I was told. Within minutes, I was unclothed and alone in a dark room.

I could feel him approach me. I smelled his stale breath and heard his heavy breathing. He began playing with my hair and touching my chest, brushing his lips over me.

When he jumped up onto the table and got on top of me, my panicked thoughts grew quietly determined. *If I don't do something now, he's going to rape me.* I began to shout and felt as though I were screaming for my life. He tried to quiet me down and cover my mouth, but I screamed louder. Shifting tactics, he shushed me and offered me money to be quiet, but I didn't stop shouting. He cursed and lunged off the table. As the security guard burst into the room, tears rolled down my cheeks, and I—still quaking—closed my eyes in quiet relief.

The doctor didn't miss a beat and nonchalantly said to the guard, "We just finished up the X-ray. I guess she feared the machine and began to shout and cry. Being a poor *Badi* girl and living in a village, she's not used to this sort of thing. But we're good here. You can go." The security guard shrugged, turned on his heels, and walked away.

As the doctor shoved me out of the room, he growled, "Your appointment is over, *Badi* trash. You will get no X-ray, no medicine, and no treatment. It's too bad. You will die a worthless *kukur* (dog)." He slammed the door shut behind me.

As I stood alone in the hallway, my legs buckled under me, and I realized the wheelchair was still in the X-ray room. But there was no way I would go back to get it, with *him* still inside. In a daze, I unsteadily and slowly shuffled to the waiting room. Finding my *buba*, I told him it was time to go home. My dad was understandably confused. "But what about your medicine, what about your treatment? We have the money for it—why aren't you using it?" Numb, I just shook my head and told him we needed to go.

After an hour on the bus, I told him what had happened. As I spoke and the distance grew between the doctor and us, I grew more angry and less afraid. My jaw tightened, and I declared, "*Buba*, we have to do something about this! It is not right, Dad." I saw his eyes well up with emotion as he shook his head. "Hannah, *chhori*. What to do, my daughter? This is what happens to us *Badi*—there is nothing we can do about it."

As I heard his words, the fire and anger in me were extinguished. I felt worn out, utterly defeated, and weak. I put my head on his shoulder and silently cried myself to sleep.

After that, I got sicker. I whispered and mumbled, struggling to speak. Soon, I grew unable to talk at all. In the evenings, my dad would put a damp towel on my face, hoping to relieve the knotted and contorted muscles. I was barely able to get out of bed, and I slept for much of the day. Most days were filled with intense physical struggle; in fact, it would be many years before I would grow stronger and be able to live free from pain.

Later that month, my cousin—my mom's nephew—came to visit. I had never liked him. One evening, I woke up with a shock to hear him breathing heavily and felt his hands all over me. He had a wild look in his eyes, and he was trying to loosen my clothes. I screamed. My mom burst into the room, and when she saw what was happening, she shouted, "You must go … now! You are never again welcome here!" As he left our house that night, I was more convinced than ever that men were dangerous.

Though neither the doctor nor my cousin raped me, their entitled attitudes to do as they pleased—in the hospital and in my home—left a mark. The grip of fear and anger grew tighter still, and I determined that men were not to be trusted.

Over-promising and Under-delivering

I was born a question-asker and boundary-breaker. "You're the most curious animal in the world," my *aama* would say. Generally, if someone told me not to do something, it made me want to do it. Ever since I was little, I have been a fighter.

In my culture, lighter skin is deemed more attractive. One day, I heard a neighbor tell my parents, "Hannah's skin is too dark. She will never be beautiful." Men taunted me and called me ugly. I was angry and shouted back at them. It didn't matter if they were bigger and stronger than me; I would hurl stones at them and demand that they stop. Some people in my village found my strong spirit entertaining, shaking their heads and chuckling. Others thought I just needed to stop resisting and be quiet. (That was *never* going to happen.)

It was probably this curiosity and fiery nature that caused me to race and try to be the first to welcome the few outsiders who came to visit. I was eager to see what brought them to our remote village, in the middle of a dense jungle, with the nearest town an hour's drive away. Sometimes men came with marriage proposals, and other times, a government or Nepali NGO offered livelihood or development programs to help our community. (NGO is an acronym for a nongovernmental organization—a nonprofit operating independently of any government.)

NGOs had a reputation among the *Badi* for coming in to "help" and then leaving after just a few months. A few times during my childhood, they rumbled down the steep hill to our remote village, wiping the dust off their nice clothes as they got out of their SUVs. Sometimes they wore kind expressions, and at other times, troubled or condescending looks. No doubt, it was evident to them that we were impoverished and struggling to survive.

I did whatever I could to give them what they wanted: a tour of the village, an introduction to our elders, or a smile for their pictures. I preferred touring and introducing them, but if someone else beat me to it, I trailed closely behind and listened to what they were saying as they walked or sat to speak to the village leaders.

I remember when one NGO came in and offered to build a well for us. "Why not?" said the leader of our village. For a few months, it made life interesting and rather exciting, as tractors and workmen came and went to construct the well. The day it was finished, they had a ribbon-cutting ceremony and—as always—took pictures of us children.

I'm sure they meant well, but behind their cloud of SUV dust, they left us without any instructions for how to care for or repair the well. It broke a few months later, and we had no idea how to fix it. So, we returned to collecting our water from the river. When the

NGO returned a year later to check on the well and found it covered with leaves and dust, although I didn't understand all of what they said, I saw that they were frustrated. They judged us for not using the well. Their patronizing looks said it all: *You people just don't want help. We'll go find someone more deserving, more ready for our help.*

It seemed to me that most visitors generally over-promised and under-delivered. Now, as I look back at what they offered us, I chuckle and think, *If these people had followed through with all their promises, our village would look like New York City.*

But no ... very little changed for us in the wake of their projects and their promises to help. Our young girls were still disappearing and being trafficked, we were still landless, there were still no opportunities to go to school, and many were still dying because of the lack of access to medicine, food, and clean water.

But all of that changed in 2009 when two men came to visit.

Gamble of a Lifetime (2009)

When they walked into our village—as was often the case—I was the first to greet the two newcomers. Little did I know that, at fourteen years old, this was a meeting that would alter the course of my life.

My curiosity was immediately piqued because these men didn't look wealthy, like many of the other visitors who came to our village. In fact, they both looked *garib* (poor), just like us. They were not wearing fancy suits but were dressed simply in sweatpants, T-shirts, and flip-flops. I asked for their names and learned that one man, named Raju, was Nepali. When I heard that his friend, Håkan, was from Sweden—the first foreigner to ever visit our village—I became even *more* interested. I wondered, *What do they want, and what are they doing here?*

I offered them a tour of our village, and after the tour, Raju asked me, "Hannah, can we talk with you and your parents for a little bit?" I took them to my house, and as they offered my mom and dad our customary way of saying hello, "*Namaste*" (Greetings), it struck me how respectfully they spoke. This was most uncommon, and I became even more intrigued.

As the sun's light faded and our faces glowed with the fire's light, the two men shared their stories and what led them to visit us. In no time, it seemed, the whole village had gathered to sit and listen.

Raju spoke openly. He told us that he was also a *Dalit*, an *untouchable*. While his social standing was a little higher in the caste hierarchy than ours, he talked with honesty about the ways in which he, too, had experienced struggles in life due to caste. "I have often been excluded because of being *Dalit*. I have been told that I'm nothing, that I'm worthless." He continued, "I know it's even harder for you, as *Badi*. I know that you are called *the dust of Nepal* and *the untouchables of the untouchables*."

He spoke what was true—*satya*—for us, unlike any outsider had ever done before. He told us that twenty years earlier, he had watched a documentary about the struggles of the *Badi*. "As I watched it, something in me awoke, and I believed that one day I would be here, with you. I committed to doing what I could to make life better for the *Badi*. I had no idea how I would do so, but as a man of faith, I began praying every day to one day meet you. Sitting with you here tonight has been a dream of mine for twenty years."

My parents and our villagers were quiet, at times looking at each other in wonder, but mostly they listened intently to Raju. He went on and told us how, when he met Håkan a few months earlier, they quickly discovered they had a shared commitment and passion to do what they could to make life better for those most marginalized in the world. When Raju shared what he'd learned about the *Badi*, Håkan was intrigued, and they determined to travel together to the far west of Nepal to meet us.

Håkan then spoke a bit, while Raju translated, "Education has been shown to be one of the most impactful ways to create change and opportunity. We want to invite some of your children to come to

Kathmandu later this year. We are about to begin building a school and dormitory that will provide education, security, and community for *Badi* children, beginning first with your girls. Soon, we'll have room for your boys too. Does this interest you? We understand it will take time to build trust and allow us to care for your children so far away. What questions do you have for us?" I couldn't remember a time anyone had ever spoken to us with such humility and asked us our opinions.

These were two firsts I would not ever forget.

They asked if they could return the next day to talk some more. I was excited to look around the circle and see many nods of agreement. As they walked to their car, Raju paused, turned around to our group, and asked, "Is it true that men crawl through the windows of your homes, expecting to have sex with your daughters and wives—and even your grandmothers?"

A few people murmured, "*Ho*" (Yes). What they had been told was true.

The visitors gazed at us with tears in their eyes. I didn't see the looks of pity that I'd seen in other outsiders. Instead, I saw compassion and kindness.

When I went to bed that night, sleep was elusive. It had been five years since my ill-fated trip to the hospital, and at first, I thought that maybe it was the persistent pain in my body that kept me awake. But on this night, it was something else. I tossed and turned, wondering if these men would really return the following day and make good on their promise, or if it would be another story of under-delivering outsiders.

The next afternoon, I was ecstatic to see that they did, indeed, return. Again, most of the village gathered around, and the men asked us what questions we children had for them, what concerns the parents had about their children, and what our village most needed. For the remainder of the afternoon, we mostly spoke, and they mostly listened.

When we asked Håkan, "What brought you to us?" he told us about a friend of his in a country not too far from us, in Myanmar, who had lived as a slave on a fishing boat for eight years before he was able to escape. His voice quiet and eyes thoughtful, he said, "This friend planted a seed of a dream in me to one day be able to help others who are also at risk of being enslaved. I know that many of your girls are trafficked and are slaves in brothels." As he spoke, again, he had tears in his eyes, and his voice cracked with emotion.

In that moment, the whispers and talking that had been going on among the hundreds of villagers who had gathered around fell silent. I don't know what they were feeling, but I was in awe. Once again, his story and tears seemed genuine. This man seemed to really care about his fisherman friend in Myanmar *and* about us. My heart was touched, and I was curious: *Might these men be trustworthy?*

As the day turned to night, someone began to play music. Before long, others joined, and our village took on the air of a festival celebration. My *aama* begged me to dance—my mom has always loved to watch me dance. The other villagers pleaded, "Dance, Hannah." As I looked at my *buba*, he said, "*Chhori*, do what you want."

I smiled with eagerness. Truth be told, it rarely took much convincing for me to dance. This night was no exception. I felt proud as my feet pounded the ground, and I spun with abandon and dramatic flourish. It wasn't often we were able to perform for people outside our village. But when Raju stood up and asked for the music to stop, the *madal*-drums fell silent, and I stopped twirling.

He spoke with tenderness, directly to me. "We are not here to see you dance, Hannah. Although your dancing is beautiful, you do not need to perform for us. We want nothing from you. We are the ones who have something to offer you: an education and a future."

The villagers seemed both surprised and doubtful. I heard someone whisper, "I don't believe they came here merely to offer education to our children. Why would they do this for us without expecting anything in return?"

I, too, had so many questions. In the back of my mind, I thought that surely these two men had come for the same reason all other men came: for entertainment, and ultimately, for sex.

But I was filled with hope and longing. I wondered, *What if they are telling the truth, and I could go to school?* They were right—education *did* create empowerment and opportunity. And going to school *was* my biggest dream.

I felt a flutter of possibility at the prospect that this dream of mine might come true. While I wasn't going to blindly follow or trust these men—for, I reminded myself, *Men are dangerous!*—I decided to stay cautiously open to what could be an opportunity of a lifetime.

As they walked up the hill leading out of our village, they promised to return and not forget about us.

Faithful to his promise, Raju returned regularly that year. He told us that Håkan had left Nepal to raise funds for the school and dormitory. Raju continued to ask questions and listen to what we most needed. When he heard that we were hungry, he brought rice … and a first for most of us, chocolate. When he heard that my friends and I wanted to learn to write, he brought pencils and paper—also a first. As much as we loved the chocolates, the paper and pencils made us even happier!

He never told us that he would buy us land or build fancy houses or wells. He planted one seed, one seed only, in our hearts: education. He always gave us updates about the construction process and made us feel that we were a part of the project. During one visit, he showed us pictures of the scaffolding of the school and dormitory. On the next visit, he said that the buildings were almost finished and that there would soon be room for thirty girls to go to school in Kathmandu.

When he left, my friends and I, along with our parents, often talked about our excitement and concerns, especially having to live so far away to attend school. I found myself waffling between the risk and the reward. I knew if I stayed, education was unlikely. Without it, there was very little chance for a future with any possibility. And yet, I was wary. Men and women, family and friends, government and nonprofit organizations had all offered proposals that would make life better for us. Usually, the result was disappointing, providing us with little to nothing of value.

My parents said that the choice was up to me. When December arrived and Raju returned, thirty-three girls and I had made our decision. Together, with my niece Bina, it was our turn to drive away on the dusty road and head by bus on a twenty-hour journey to Kathmandu.

While I felt in my gut that this was a risk worth taking, only time would tell if this gamble of a lifetime would pay off.

Introductions: Our Storytellers

Let me introduce you to the others in this story. My mom's name is Maya. Meena is my eldest sister, followed by my sister Aasha. Sakhira and Khushi are not my biological sisters, but we call each other sisters nonetheless. That's just how we are in Nepal; we speak of one another as our family, including those outside of our "blood" family.

When Sarah *didi* and I decided it was time to begin this book, I took Aasha, Sakhira, and Khushi out to a café in Kathmandu. (Meena was at home in our village, taking care of our *aama*, so she joined via phone.) We got brownies and coffee ice cream—a first-time treat for my friends and sister. We talked together for four hours, lingering over spoonfuls of decadent dessert and conversation. I shared with them my dream for this book and my excitement that it might be the first one published in English about the *Badi*. We discussed how they felt about sharing their stories.

I invited them to join this project because I know them well and love each one of them with all my heart, and I believe their stories—each one—are important and powerful. But they don't see themselves the way I see them. I told them, "I know that you've been told for your whole life that you are nothing. But each one of you is important. Each one of you has a story the world needs to hear. Whether you say *ho* or no, I believe that you are each a glittering and beautiful diamond."

My friend Sakhira laughed and lightly teased, "Glittering and beautiful diamonds? Oh, Hannah, you do have a crazy way with words!" She then grew serious and voiced her concerns, "But what will people think of me when they read my story? No one knows my whole story. I worry it will bring shame to my family to share it." Khushi and Aasha nodded in agreement.

Wordlessly, we sat quietly together for a few minutes. I understood their fears about how our families and community would respond. It also got me thinking. People often speak of Nepal as a *shame-based culture*. But the more I travel the world, the more I think that people all over the world struggle with shame too. It is not just a *Nepali thing*. It is a *human thing*. To be a truth-teller about personal struggles is not easy.

I shared my musings with my sisters. As I talked and as we sat together, I grew more convinced about how powerful and important it was that this story be told *now*. "The struggles of our people will continue as long as they are hidden and remain in the dark. If we speak up, it might just bring change that is needed. It might make life better for many of our own people—and, I hope, for many in the world who also struggle and are not yet free." Pausing, I took a breath and continued, "Sisters, I believe that when we tell these stories together, it will bring us healing and make us freer than ever before."

As we sat and talked long into the afternoon, one by one, they each said, "*Ho!*" It was a unanimous *yes*. I emailed Sarah that night and told her that all five of us were *in*. Right away, we began to schedule our video interviews for the coming months.

We had our first call two weeks later. We always started with inspiration and encouragement. Sometimes we watched or listened to a song or read something aloud that we loved. Then, we would dive right in. Sarah would ask questions, listen, and type as I translated what my sisters spoke.

I believed I knew their stories before we began our interviews. But no—I quickly discovered that what they had experienced was more horrifying and traumatic than I previously understood. As they shared, there were moments when my sisters were overwhelmed, and sometimes their bodies would tremble uncontrollably. When that happened, we would stop and just be quiet or whisper a prayer for courage. Ultimately, our love for each other and our faith gave us just enough strength to move forward, even with racing hearts.

As you read the stories of my brave and heroic sisters, I hope you come to love them too.

Meena: The Phoenix Rising

A Marriage Proposal (1988)

I sat with Hannah and our *aama*. I knew our mom's life had been hard from the beginning. But there was much I never understood until she shared more of her story with us. Smiling at us with love in her eyes, she began.

"One day, when I was twelve years old, a man knocked on our door. As I hid out of sight and listened to what he wanted, he told my dad that he wanted to marry me. After he left, I begged my father to say no. I did not want to get married yet.

"My *buba* looked at me for a moment and said, 'Okay, I'll tell him no. My *chhori*, I have never had a good feeling about this guy anyway—let's wait for someone better.' When your *hajurbuba* (grandfather) told him no and the man heard that I didn't want to marry him, he was furious … and undeterred."

Our *aama* looked directly at us. Her voice soft and sad, she asked, "Are you sure you want to hear the whole story? Because this part is hard." Hannah and I glanced at each other and then back to our mom, both nodding.

Inhaling deeply, *Aama* continued, "This bad man, still angry at being turned down, kept an eye on me. It was scary and unnerving. He would spy on me as I went about my work in the village. One day, as I walked to the river to do laundry, he followed me. Once out of sight of the village, he grabbed me. As I faced him, I saw his eyes flash with rage. He began to beat me and then pushed me down to the ground." Our mom shuddered, clenching her fists. "I tried to fight him with all my might, but he was stronger. I screamed at the top of my lungs, but no one heard me. That day, he raped me. My daughters, it was terrible."

Hannah asked Mom if she ever told anyone what happened. *Aama* shook her head no. "I never did, no. I was too afraid … and too ashamed."

Looking at me, she said, "Meena, my stomach began to swell. I was pregnant … with you. When my father heard that I was expecting a baby, he didn't ask any questions. It was simple in his mind and in our culture. 'That man is now your husband,' he told me. 'You must go and join his household. It's your duty, my daughter. You don't have a choice.'"

Mom lamented wistfully, "What choice did I have, but to do as he said? At twelve years old, I was pregnant and forced to become the third wife of the man who raped me."

She told us that her husband's other wives and children treated her badly from the very beginning. They made her life miserable and forced her to do the worst work, the hardest work.

With a furrowed brow, she continued, "Meena, I gave birth to you alone in the jungle. When I carried you back and collapsed in the house, the wives shouted at me to get up and make rice for their children. That day, I decided that as soon as I was strong enough, I'd leave. I didn't want you to grow up in that home, and I worried what would happen to you if we stayed."

"Two weeks later, I gathered you into my arms … and ran away. I was on my own with a baby. Now I was—we were—more vulnerable than ever."

As our *aama* closed her eyes and paused for a moment to collect herself, Hannah took my mom's hand gently in hers and whispered,

"*Aama,* we are honored to hear your story. I'm so sorry. Your life has been harder than we ever knew." My sister, *Aama,* and I sat together quietly. It was a lot to take in.

And yet, I knew it. My life was no easier … by many accounts, it had been even harder than my *aama's.*

The Tractor Men (1997)

By the time I was four years old, my mom had married and had to flee—yet again—a second abusive husband. She then met a man who promised to take care of us. While I hoped he would treat us well, I was not optimistic. We moved to his little village, called Nayagau.

He did his best, but our lives were still very difficult. With this man, my mom had six children, including my sisters Hannah and Aasha. To make a few extra *rupees* for food, our *aama* carried stone slabs of slate from the sides of the river up the steep hill to the road, high above our village. Each day, she returned home sweaty, dusty, and bone-tired. Some nights, we would have a meal, and on other nights, we would drink boiled water for dinner.

It pained me to watch her suffer so much. One day, I had the idea that it might be easier for her if I went to stay with my *hajur-buba.* I'd always had a special connection with my grandfather, and I figured it would be one less mouth for my mom to feed.

When I told my *aama* my plan, she was not convinced it was a good idea. "Meena, his village is a few hours away from ours. How will you get there?" I wasn't sure either, but I persisted. Day in and day out, I asked her to let me go. One day, a man named Ram, who was married to the sister of my cousin, heard us talking, and he said, "What a coincidence! I am heading to Surkhet, a town just one hour from here. Your grandfather's village of Ramghat is not far from there. Meena, you can come with me, and I will take you to him after I finish my business in Surkhet. It is no problem for me."

I couldn't believe it, but my *aama* agreed. I packed my things, and we left the next day. I was very young to be traveling so far from home at just nine years old, but for much of my life, my mom had needed to work long hours, and I had learned to look after myself and had become quite independent.

I'm not going to lie. I also looked forward to being freed from caring for my six siblings for a while. So, as Ram and I walked up the hill to get to the road bound for Surkhet, I was excited and very eager for the break.

We walked for about an hour and were lucky to hitch a ride the rest of the way, entering the town of Surkhet that evening. The town was aglow as the sun set. The shop windows were lit and vibrant with colorful fabrics, the *chiya* stalls steamed with aromatic vats of tea, and a few wealthy-looking and well-dressed people were walking, eating, and buzzing through town on motorcycles. How different was this world from life in my dusty village by the riverbed!

The next morning, two friends of Ram's met us for *chiya*. As we sat and sipped our tea, watching the city awaken, the men talked about their plans for the day. The two new men offered to take me to my grandfather's house, since they said they were heading that way anyway. Feeling shy and because it didn't matter much to me how I got there, I remained quiet. Plus, I was preoccupied and excitedly watched the early-morning activity around us. Shopkeepers began to open their shops, and children walked by on their way to school. The street sounds grew louder with the hum of motors from rickshaws and motorcycles.

After his last sip of *chiya*, Ram turned to me and said, "Alright, it's time for you to go see that *hajurbuba* of yours, Meena. My friends will make sure you get to your grandfather safely."

The two men and I made our way through the city and came to a large tractor. Its wheels were huge, much taller than me, and its yellow color gleamed brightly in the sun. One of the brothers said, "Get up, little one. This is our ride."

I had never ridden on a tractor before. As I climbed my way up to the seat, they let me sit next to the driver. I felt proud—almost like a princess—and held my head high as the motor roared to life and we drove out of town, making our way to my grandfather's house. How surprised my *hajurbuba* would be, not only to see me, but for me to arrive at his door atop this impressive tractor!

As we roared down the road, I began to get very sleepy. I laid my head down on the rumbling cushion, lulled asleep by the motor and a stomach full of spicy milk *chiya*.

When I woke up, it was dark. I was no longer on the tractor. In fact, there was no tractor in sight. As I looked around, I found myself in a home I didn't recognize. It was not my grandfather's home. *Where am I?* I wondered. In the next room, I heard a language I didn't understand very well, but I recognized it as *Hindi*, the language of northern India.

One of the tractor men came into the room speaking Nepali. "Get up, Meena! Make us some dinner!" My mind reeled. *Where am I, who am I cooking for, and where is my grandfather?* He must have seen my confusion, saying, "We paid lots of money for you to Ram. You belong to us now. Do as we say. Nepal is far from here, so do not dare to try and run away. Right now, we are hungry, so make us some food."

As he pushed me into the kitchen, tears rolled down my cheeks. This was not a good situation. At nine years old, I was in a country that wasn't my own. I didn't speak the language. And my family had no idea where I was. I had no choice but to do as I was told.

A Blur of Three Years (1997-2000)

The next three years were a blur. I worked from sunrise until late at night. I cooked, cleaned, did laundry, and took care of the household's many young children. I did whatever the men and their wives wanted. The two brothers—I called them the *tractor men*—and another brother lived together in this home. These three men took turns taking me to their bedrooms where they forced me to have sex with them night after night.

One of the brothers began to fall in love with me ... or so he said. He told me that I was special and beautiful. He promised to take good care of me and buy me nice clothes and jewelry. When he spoke, his breath was stale with alcohol, his words slurred, and his eyes were blurry.

I did not love or trust this tractor man. But when I became pregnant, I loved my *chhora* (son). I was eleven years old when Anas—meaning *love and affection*—was born. I stayed awake at night just to listen to him breathe and basked in the feeling of him cuddling close to me. He grew so fast and learned new words each day. To me, he was the smartest, most handsome boy in the world.

When my beautiful *chhori*, Bina, was born one year later, she made my life brighter, but having my second child made me even more homesick. I wanted my children to know their aunties and grandparents and to play with their cousins by the river. I dreamed of being safely away from these men, their sex demands at night, and the never-ending work requirements of their household.

When one of the wives attempted to murder my daughter, I decided it was no longer just a dream to get out of there. I *had* to figure out a way to get home.

Here's what happened: One day, as I entered the kitchen to begin preparing lunch, I saw the wife of one of the tractor men crouched quietly over Bina. I knew she was up to no good—I could feel it in my bones. As I pushed her aside, I saw that she held a handful of rice hulls and was about to put them down my baby's throat.

If I hadn't stopped her, the razor-sharp hulls would have slit Bina's throat. These hulls—or husks—are part of the chaff of rice, and in much of Asia, they are used as fertilizer, insulation, fuel, and building material. On this day, they were about to be used for another purpose: to kill my daughter. I had heard stories of why this was done ... it was a cheap way to get rid of unwanted baby girls. I believed this family wanted Bina dead since girls are considered expensive in India because of their dowry—or bride price. Still today, this is done. Girls are often poisoned, suffocated, or starved to death. But Bina was *my baby girl.* I knew I *had to* get her out of there if she were to survive.

I saw my opportunity one day while I was getting vegetables at the market with Bina swaddled and tightly strapped to my back. I heard my language. It was not just the language of Nepali, but was *Khamsi,* the language of my people, the *Badi.*

I was shy and fearful. With my heart beating through my chest, I willed myself to approach the two women who were speaking *Khamsi* and ask them for help. My words tumbled over one another as I told them my story as quickly as I could. I begged them to help me communicate with my family back in Nepal. There was a little shop behind us that sold postcards. They bought a postcard and wrote my message as I spoke: "I am alive. I have a *chhora,* Anas, and a newborn *chhori,* Bina. I am living in Rupaidiha, India. I'm very unhappy. I need your help and want to come home." I included the names of the three men and hoped they could find the home where I lived.

As the women put a stamp on the postcard, I doubted that this little piece of paper would even make it to my little-known village by the river in the far west of Nepal. But what was there to lose in trying? This might be my only chance.

A Knock on the Door (2000)

One morning, just two months later, I was making breakfast. The kitchen was fragrant with lemon and curry leaves as I stirred onions and potatoes into the flattened rice. I heard a knock on the door, and soon after, I heard a voice I recognized. My stepfather had found me! This was the first glimpse of hope I'd had in three years.

He was very clever. Although he knew I was unhappy and that this was a dangerous place for my children and me, my stepfather did not convey any of this to the tractor men. No, he knew how to speak to them in a smart and convincing way. "This is a beautiful house! The gods must be pleased with you, as your destiny is good! My daughter is lucky to live in such a magnificent house. And you know what? I have other daughters who are also beautiful and good workers. I will give you a good price for them."

Then he said, "Please, her mother misses her so very much and would love to meet her grandchildren. Would you allow her to come home to celebrate our next festival with us? After she returns to you, we can talk about my other daughters." The tractor brothers seemed interested and told him they would think about it.

Giving a good price for daughters likely sounds strange to some, but in much of Nepal and India, it is very, very common. In our *Badi* community, girls are bought and sold all the time. In fact, when a man has many daughters, it is said about him, "Oh, the gods have favored him. He is a lucky one and will be rich!" But being born into my family made me a *lucky one* because my parents were different. Their destitution did not compel them to look at us as property to be sold. They chose to go hungry rather than sell their girls for *rupees*.

As the tractor brothers went outside to smoke, my stepfather found me in the kitchen. Looking around to make sure no one was near, he whispered to me, "Meena, don't worry—I'll find a way. I must go back to Nepal now, but don't worry. You will be back with us soon. Trust me."

A week later, I heard the men talking about my stepfather's offer to sell his other daughters. One of the men said, "Ram told me they are very beautiful, like Meena. They could make us rich. Let's let Meena go home—and see what price her family offers us for his other daughters."

So, for the *Dishain* festival, the longest and most auspicious festival in Nepal, they allowed my children and me to go home for three weeks. On the two-and-a-half-day bus ride home, I was breathless with excitement. Yet I was also afraid of the days ahead. *What would happen next?* I did not want to return to the house of the tractor men, but I wasn't sure I had a choice—I might have to go back, whether I wanted to or not.

A Devastating Twist of Fate (2000)

A few days later, I sat with my *aama* and sipped *chiya* in my village home as my children played happily on their grandma's lap. My little sisters surrounded us. I told them everything—from the time I left our village three years ago until returning that very day. They hung on every word of my story.

With tears in her eyes, my *aama* promised, "Meena, we will protect you."

But I *was* worried. The men knew where I came from and would know right where to find me. My stepdad was one step ahead of me, though, and he'd made plans to hide me in a nearby village with his *dai* (elder brother), safely out of sight of our curious neighbors. He knew they would come for me. And he was right.

Two weeks after I was supposed to return to India, my family told me that the tractor brothers came rumbling down the road, pulling the tractor to the side of the road at the top of our village hill, high above the river. They were angry and forcibly banged on the door of our home. They pounded and demanded that *their property*—me—be returned, saying, "We paid lots of money for her and she *belongs to us!*"

Gathering men from my village, my stepdad stood nose to nose with the angry men and told them, "No! She is not yours. We know what happened. We know that you drugged and kidnapped her, that she's been a slave to your household. We know that you have been forcing her to have sex. We will not give her back. And we have already notified the police. So leave. Leave our village now!"

And leave, they did. They were an enraged, buzzing swarm of flies as they stormed up the hill. They couldn't believe that we, being

Badi, the dust of Nepal, would dare to stand up to them and report them to the police.

But that day, as he thundered up the hill, the father of my son did something that would forever change my life. I can barely tell it. But tell it, I will. My son, Anas, was sitting by the river with some other children. When my boy's father recognized him, he sprinted to the riverside, snatched him up, and took him to where the rumbling tractor awaited. He left, carrying our son away from me in a triumphant cloud of dust.

My *aama* came to the village where I was hiding to tell me that the men had come and gone. She began crying and told me that my boy had been taken.

I screamed. I cried. I wailed. I pounded the dirt. I returned to my village, sitting in the dark of my mom's home, as if in a fog. "My son is gone. He is only one—no one can take care of him like me! I want him back. I cannot bear to be without him."

My heart was torn in two. A deep sense of despair took hold of me, and I lost the will to do anything. I floated through my days adrift in an ocean of grief ... I wanted to die. We could not go back to India to get Anas. They would surely kill me, my stepfather, or anyone who dared to try.

There was nothing I or anyone else could do to bring Anas back. I have not seen my boy since.

Deceived Again (2002)

I was thankful to be back in my village, *ho*. I loved my *chhori*, Bina, yes. I tried to enter back into the life of our village, spending the days with my sisters and caring for Bina. But underneath it all, I was restless and depressed. My heart ached with worry about my son.

As I was doing laundry by the river one day, a woman from our village, named Chaha, approached me. She said that she would be going to India soon. "You can come with me, if you want." She piqued my curiosity with stories of plenty: *rupees*, clothes, jewelry, and food. "You can send money home to your family and to Bina."

Chaha warned me not to tell my parents. "They will say you are too young, at fourteen, to leave the village again. But if you can't make money, Bina may see the same fate as you: hungry and with no future, she will be vulnerable to traffickers. Really, what kind of life is here for you or her?"

As she spoke, my throat tightened with emotion. Chaha was right. If I wanted a different life for my daughter, I needed to do something different. If I stayed in my village, it would be the same story of struggle for her as for so many *Badi* ... with many monotonous and meaningless days, year after year.

With my son gone and my baby girl's future in mind, I decided to make a new start and create a new life that would be better for both of us. I said *hunchha*. Yes, I would go. Chaha told me she had a plan and instructed me to be ready to go when she said it was time. A few days later, we went into the jungle to collect firewood. Once out of sight of the village, she said, "Meena, let's go to India!" We began to run.

I didn't even say goodbye to my family. I felt ashamed—yet I had worried that my parents would, as Chaha said, keep me from going. As I ran, I fled the pain of losing my son and the fear of my daughter's fate being as hopeless as mine. I ran toward a new life. I hoped to be able to make money to send home to my parents and Bina. I planned to return as soon as I could.

We made our way to New Delhi, the capital of India. I was in awe. The town in India where I had lived before was small—nothing like the clamor, the noise, the smells, and the press of people I found in Delhi.

As we entered a busy marketplace, Chaha led me to a place that was unlike anywhere I'd seen before. I didn't like it ... no, not at all. She first led me up two dark stairways, and then we entered a dimly lit hallway.

As we walked past gated concrete-walled rooms with large metal doors secured by bolts from the outside, I saw dozens of girls inside the rooms. Some slept, some were putting on makeup, but they were all *locked inside* the rooms. The sights and sounds of sex were everywhere.

My voice shaky, I told Chaha, "I don't like this place. If this is where you want me to *work*, I want to go someplace else." It was a bad place, dark with dread and fear. I could feel it. She didn't say anything in response but only looked at me over her shoulder with a sneer and kept walking. *What else could I do but follow her? So much for better choices.*

Chaha introduced me to the *ma'am*, the *boss* of the brothel. The promise of a *fresh start* was not a good one as the *ma'am* began to speak. "You ran through the jungle to get here, right?" I nodded, looking at the floor. "Well, then, your family probably thinks a wild animal ate you in the jungle after you left. There is no way they know that you're in New Delhi now. So don't fight it. You will stay here and work. You must. There is no other place for you to go, no other way for you to make money, no other way to stay alive."

Her eyes gleamed with unnerving pleasure. "Don't worry, Meena. You are pretty, and one of your *customers* might fall in love with you and take care of you. Sometimes that happens … if you're lucky."

A tall and strong man appeared in the doorway and led me down the hall. We stopped at a room crowded with girls. They were behind bars; it looked just like a prison. He shoved me into the barred room, securing the lock behind me.

I found an empty corner, squatted down, and wept. *What am I doing here? What am I going to do?* In that dark corner, exhausted and overwhelmed, I leaned my head against the wall and nodded off. I was roused from my sleep by someone shouting my name. The big man was hollering, and his eyes glared at me. "Meena. Meena, wake up! You have a *customer*."

A customer. Very quickly, I came to know very well what *that* meant. Night after night, year after year, these *customers* came. They each came for the same thing: sex.

I came to know that Chaha was one of the pimps of this place. I was now being kept behind locked bars in a brothel on G.B. Road in one of New Delhi's red-light districts.

At first, my thoughts were consumed with how to get out and return to my daughter and family in Nepal. But in time, I began to believe this nightmare was my fate and saw no way out.

"Work Old" (2007)

By the time I was nineteen, I had been living on G.B. Road for five years and pregnant nine times. At the first sign of my stomach swelling, I was taken to a place in the city where they ripped my babies out, one after another.

I came to know this dark and ugly room well.

Each time I got pregnant, I cried. I begged. I pleaded to keep each one but was told, "No, Meena, no. Babies are bad for business." But finally, at the end of my fifth year in the brothel, the *ma'am* said she *might* let me keep "this one." When she called me in to talk with her about being pregnant, I figured it would be like every other time. But this day, it was different. She told me, "You are now 'work old,' Meena. Men like young girls more than old ones. It's time for a change for you."

Truth be told, I felt *old*. I was tired. My body pained me everywhere. In my years of work in the past nearly half-dozen years, sometimes fifteen, twenty, thirty *customers* came to me each night—on busy nights, it was as many as sixty men. I had no days off, ever. By my estimation, conservatively speaking, I'd been with at least fifty thousand men thus far … too many, that's for sure. My body had been a revolving door, forcibly made to have sex with men young and old, rich and poor, foreign and local.

The *ma'am* took me to a clinic to determine the gender of my baby. When she heard it was a girl, the *boss* looked at me and said, "*Hunchha*, yes, you can keep this baby." I was elated … and at the same time, I wondered what my *chhori*, Bina, now seven years old, was up to in Nepal and how my eight-year-old boy, Anas, was faring with those terrible tractor brothers in India.

I was moved to Meerut, India, which is about two hours from G.B. Road, where "work old" women like me lived. I still *worked*. My regular *customers* came to me or sent rickshaws for me that took me to a hotel to meet them.

Some women from this house were hired by cruise ships and resorts as call girls. Some men booked women three or four months in advance before a trip to New Delhi. If they really liked a girl, they would fly her to meet them on vacation. But not me. I was never chosen to leave this place. Now that I was pregnant, it would probably not ever happen—which was fine with me.

So, there I was, "work old" at nineteen, pregnant, and worried about the world into which my daughter would soon make her entrance. I was made to work day and night, even as my belly grew. I worked until the day my baby girl was born.

When my daughter was born, I named her Kaya. Just holding her and looking at her made my world feel new. Being with her made me happy. The day after she was born, the *ma'am* came to visit. Kaya was fair-skinned, and because of that, the *ma'am* declared her to be very beautiful. She handed me a gift—a package of makeup, clothing, and jewelry. As I held the package in my hand, she declared that she had given it to me so that I could start freshening up for one of my regular *customers* who would be sending for me in a few hours.

I wasn't ready. My body hurt from delivering my baby the day before. I was tired, so very tired. I didn't want to leave Kaya alone in this place. I asked for more time.

The *boss* was infuriated and picked up a razor. She pushed Kaya aside and began slashing my breasts and screaming, "I hope this teaches you who is the *boss*. You have repaid your debt, *ho*. You are free to leave, yes. But if you decide to leave, you cannot take your daughter. And if you stay, you must work. These breasts are here to make money, not to feed that baby girl. Don't forget it. I allowed you to work less and to give birth to your baby, but *she is not yours*. No, Meena, *she belongs to me.*"

My mind went blank. Blank. Dark. *What have I done? I can now leave, but Kaya cannot? What kind of life is this for my baby girl?*

There was nothing to do but go back to work. The other women in the brothel told me that my baby girl cried all night when I was gone that first night. She was hungry. I'd known hunger my whole life, but it tore my heart in two to know that my little baby was hungry too. I'd been enslaved here for many years, but never did I feel so hopeless, so lost, and so heartbroken. There was nothing to do but do as I was told.

The house in which we now lived was no good. It was not a good place to raise a child. Parts of the roof were missing, and rain poured into the house when the monsoons dropped their never-ending buckets of water from the sky. Just outside its doors were other homes made of scraps of tin, cardboard, and plastic. Called a "slum" by some, it was a dangerous, dirty, and dark place. I hated myself for bringing her into this world. I began cutting myself on the inside of my wrists. The pain and despair were too much to bear.

From the moment she was born, the adult world of sex and alcohol surrounded baby Kaya. She learned to crawl through the brown-red tinted *paan* spit puddles; she played with beer bottles, cigarette butts, and condoms she found on the floor. She went to sleep and woke up to the sounds of sex.

I understand it; now, I see it clearly. I was allowed to have this baby because the *ma'am* was preparing her for a future like mine. This was intentional so she would become accustomed to this way of life. My baby was being groomed to be part of the next generation of *workers*.

The next year, I had another girl, and I named her Nanu. From the very beginning, the *boss* was not as pleased with this girl as she was with Kaya. "This one is so dark-skinned. She's black and ugly, Meena. Her life is not worth much, not much at all. She is a waste."

Enraged, she slashed my breasts again with a razor. This time, I didn't even cry. I barely felt the cuts.

I wanted to die.

What could I do to change the fate of my girls? Nothing.

Once again, I had no choice.

Aasha: The Clever One

A Hard Year (2003)

My younger sister Hannah was born with big dreams for our future, especially when it came to education. Maybe it was because she was my best friend, but her big dream to be educated steadily seeped into, and eventually became, my own. As often as we could, we walked together to attend school. We rarely missed a day.

But my goodness ... it was not easy!

As *Badi* children—*the untouchables of the untouchables*—we were not wanted or welcome anywhere, including the classroom. That meant that if we were to attend school, we *had* to remain out of sight. So, here's what we did: After every student and teacher had entered the classroom and the day's lessons began, we would quietly crawl and crouch below an open-air window of the building. We would listen, craning our necks to catch as many of the teacher's words as we could. We could never look above the window's edge at what she wrote, for that would expose our position, and we did not have any supplies or books.

Over and over, we were kicked off the school property ... some days before we even made it to the window. But we were undeterred from returning day after day. As we walked and talked—there was a lot of time to talk on our five-mile walk to school—Hannah often told me how disciplined, brave, and persevering I was. She called me, "the clever one." (She's always been my greatest cheerleader.)

The truth was that life in a *Badi* village was not easy, and it required discipline, bravery, and perseverance. The insects always made themselves right at home by our riverbed. Cockroaches and spiders were numerous, but the worst and the most plentiful were the *machcharaharu* (mosquitoes). Our bodies were continuously covered with itchy, painful bites.

Many in our village got sick and died from malaria. When I was twelve, I had malaria and typhoid at the same time. "She might be a clever one, but she is also an unlucky one," the villagers whispered to each other, shaking their heads in sorrow. "She will not recover from this."

When our people, the *Badi*, get sick, we rarely have access to medicine or can be seen by a doctor. These are privileges for the rich, and the towns with hospitals are far away. Lucky for me, my dad knew a lot about natural medicine.

My sisters kept me company as my fever raged. My *aama* boiled water, and *Buba* rushed into the jungle and quickly collected some medicine of leaves and grass that he knew would treat malaria and typhoid. My dad came back, dropped them into the boiling water, and stirred it with a look of fervent intensity. He was determined to make me well. In a few minutes, he brought a steaming cup to me. With tears in his eyes, he said, "Drink, *chhori*. Daughter, may the gods spare you."

My family took turns sitting by my bedside. It took many days, but I slowly got better. Once again, my dad saved one of his girls' lives. *Hah! Maybe I am a lucky one after all!*

As I grew stronger, I began to be more active during the day and was able to do my chores. One day, after returning home with an armful of firewood from the jungle, I heard a man's voice in our home. Quietly, I put the wood on the dirt floor of our front porch and listened. He said, "*Kaka*, I love Aasha. Uncle, I want to marry her. I promise, I will give your daughter a good life—a much better one than she has now. She will not be hungry or want for anything anymore."

My dad was silent for a few moments. Slowly, he spoke. "Okay, *hunchha*. Yes, you can marry Aasha."

As the marriage proposal man left, I saw it was Garvesh. I had never liked him. His cousin, Ram, was the one who had kidnapped Meena and sold her to the tractor men. There were rumors that Garvesh had two other wives in New Delhi. Many girls in our village had left with Garvesh and never returned. I did not trust this man at all!

I walked into the house and fell at my dad's feet. "No, *Buba*, please no. I don't want to get married yet. I am only twelve years old—I don't want to be anyone's wife yet. And I do not want to marry a man like Garvesh. Look what his cousin did to Meena!"

"Aasha, what to do? Life is no good for you now. Maybe with him, it will be better. He has plenty of money. We have so little to offer you." He had made his decision. But I would not go along with it. I was determined to find a way out of this arrangement.

The next morning, Garvesh came to our home and approached me. I told him I knew what he and my father had decided the day before. "Even though my dad said *hunchha*, my answer is no. I will not marry you. Not now. Not ever."

At first, he spoke nicely, trying to convince me to change my mind. "Aasha, I love you. You're beautiful. I will take care of you." He was lying. I could see there was little truth in his words. But he did try. For a few days, he followed me everywhere and tried to convince me to marry him.

I was firm in my answer. "No, my decision is no, and I will not change my mind." While I might have been too young to know much, I did know this: Garvesh was not to be trusted, and I wanted to stay in the village with my family.

After a week, he grew angry and would shout at me as I walked to and from school with Hannah. He would not take *no* for an answer. He had his eyes on me.

One morning, I headed off early into the jungle to collect *amala* (gooseberries) for my family, hoping I could gather what I needed before the heat grew sweltering. The shade of the trees was a welcomed respite from the already warm sun. I had always liked being in the jungle, mostly because I loved climbing trees. In fact, my sisters often called me a *badar* (monkey).

I found my favorite tree and climbed as high as I could. Resting in the crook of some tall branches, I closed my eyes. I liked the feeling of being high in the trees, high above it all. In a few minutes, I knew I needed to get to my chores. Letting myself down and dropping to the jungle floor, I felt uneasy. *Is there an animal nearby?* Our jungle was full of wild animals. We had heard that a *chituwa* (leopard) had killed several people in the past year. I decided to work quickly and collected berries as fast as I could, looking over my shoulder as I did.

Suddenly, I saw him. The marriage proposal man, Garvesh, was standing not too far from me. And he was not alone. He had a friend with him. The look in their eyes sent shivers up and down my spine.

Before I even had a chance to scream, they came closer and grabbed me, covering my mouth with their hands. As he dragged me up the path to the road, Garvesh spoke, "Aasha, beautiful Aasha, you've made this hard. I tried to be nice. But now, you must do as I say and go where I tell you to go. You have no choice." There was a motorcycle parked on the road, and all three of us squeezed onto the bike. Sandwiched tightly between the two of them, we sped off in a cloud of dust. I could see we were traveling away from our village, and I wondered, *Where are they taking me?* I was terrified, but what could I do?

After a few hours, we arrived at the town of Mehelkuna. They led me to the door of a small guesthouse. As my eyes adjusted to the darkness, I saw at least a dozen other girls pressed together in the tiny room. They looked scared. Most seemed to be in their teens, like me.

Garvesh's friend grabbed my arm and pulled me to him so that his face was just inches from mine. "Don't you dare make a sound, pretty little thing." Pushing me to the ground, he snarled, "Be quiet and stay still." A few minutes later, Garvesh entered the room, bringing us sodas and steaming *dal bhat* (lentils and rice). I pushed the food away and told him I wanted to go home.

"Aasha, it's okay, don't worry. We are taking you to a place where you can make money—plenty of it. When you return to your family, you will be rich, and you can bring them gifts and food. Your family will be so proud of you." Garvesh's words were sweet like honey, but his eyes were dark.

I was in big trouble, and I knew it.

I didn't eat anything. I had no appetite, but I was thirsty, so I slowly sipped a soda. Suddenly and intensely, my eyes grew heavy. The room first became fuzzy and then went dark. When I opened my eyes, I found myself in a concrete-walled room with no windows. Bars enclosed one side of the room, alongside a hallway. I had no idea where I was. I did recognize some of the girls from the guesthouse in Mehelkuna, and they, too, seemed groggy and confused. Still tired, I fell back into a bleary sleep.

The next time I opened my eyes, I saw Garvesh staring at me from the doorway. As he came closer, I stiffened. "Aasha, beautiful one, I love you. I will take care of you. It is time now to do what married people do." He began to take off my clothes, growing angry as I screamed and begged for him to stop. I'd never been touched like this—I was just a twelve-year-old girl. I hadn't even had my first menstrual cycle yet. His eyes were dark and dangerous. I was afraid—petrified—*what could I do?* What choice did I have? He was much stronger than me. As he forced himself on me, I found mercy in a foggy blackness and passed out.

I woke up to someone shouting, "Aasha, get up! It's time to work!" I pressed my eyes hard to try to wake up. It was Garvesh. "If you work hard and do a good job, my family—the *bosses* of this place—will treat you well. But if you don't, it will not be good for you. Not good at all."

He pulled me out of the room and led me down the hallway. Rounding a corner, we came to a room with piles and piles of laundry. Soiled *saris* (a typical garment worn by women, using a long piece of fabric wrapped around the body) were piled higher than me. The room smelled of sweat and sex.

I had no choice but to become his *swasni* (wife). I soon discovered that I was right about two things: Garvesh had two other wives, and he was a very bad man. Night after night, he forced me to take drugs and drink alcohol ... and he raped me. He was rough and unkind when he was drunk and high—which was, in my memory, every single day.

My life was an endless cycle of washing giant piles of laundry and violent visits from my husband. My work had begun. I was a servant-slave to the brothel and a sex-slave to my husband. I came to learn I was living on G.B. Road in New Delhi, India. My husband and his two sisters were *bosses* and their *aama* was the *ma'am*, the big *boss* of our brothel. It was a family affair.

One night, my husband-brothel *boss* was drunk again and tearfully agitated. "We need more money. You must help us." Behind the tears, his eyes were as dark and dangerous as ever. I was worried. *What did he want me to do?*

"You are beautiful and young, Aasha, and men will pay lots of money to be with you. I can't keep you for myself any longer. My family won't allow it. I have no choice."

That night, he gave me special skin cream and products for my hair. "This is a gift from your *sasu* (mother-in-law)." The next morning, the *ma'am*—also my *sasu*—called for me. In a room reserved for her important meetings, she brushed and played with my hair, pinched my cheeks, and told me how beautiful I was. "I am proud of you, Aasha. We are happy to have you as part of our family." Her words were sweet, but her agenda was bitter. "It is time for you to make money by having sex with many men, like the other girls in this place do. We need more money, Aasha. You are part of our family now, and you must help."

After our meeting, I made my way to the laundry room. I understood. I knew I could not fight it. Tears poured from my eyes into the bucket of soapy laundry water as I washed piles of foul-smelling clothing. Soon, my *saris* would be added to the piles of sex-stained laundry. Again, my fate was sealed. It seemed that ultimately, the villagers were right about me: I was unlucky.

My husband's brown *paan* spittle had formed a long line along the walls by my bed, and soon, these walls would be covered with *paan*-spit of the never-ending flood of men who poured in and out of my bed in the brothel.

I was lost. Forgotten. Trapped.

Helpers for My Barefoot Escape (2005)

Nearly every day for a year, my mother-in-law and *ma'am* would tell me, "Aasha, if you try to escape, we will catch you. You might be a young one—just twelve years old—and my daughter-in-law, but I will beat you, and maybe, if you're unlucky, I'll kill you. Many have tried, and no one ever leaves alive. So, don't even think about it."

But I did. I thought about it every day.

And I did try.

One day, I found that a window in the bathroom was broken, and there was enough room for me to slip out. *This is my chance,* I thought. Climbing through the broken glass and stepping onto the ledge, I looked down and saw that I stood three stories above the ground. Butterflies fluttered in my stomach, and I swayed for a moment in fear. Taking a breath, I shook off the trepidation and snuck up one floor to the rooftop, where our laundry dried in the hot sun. Sure enough, there was a rainbow of *saris* gently fluttering in the breeze.

Saris vary in length, but they typically consist of six yards (eighteen feet) of material. Just to be safe, I gathered a half-dozen *saris* and then raced down one flight of stairs, eager to be out of sight of the watchful eyes of the guards. I crouched below the ledge and began to tie the *saris* together. I tied one end of the *sari* chain to a bar in the bathroom window and began to lower myself to the ground. Slowly, slowly, one hand over the other, my heart pounding with exertion and fear, I let myself down.

I didn't realize it then, but a piece of glass had sliced a nasty gash from my ankle to my knee. Blood poured from my leg to the street below as I lowered myself down. The moment my feet touched the ground, a shadow covered me, and I looked up to see the strong man of the brothel.

He sneered, "Nice try, Aasha. You've got to be smarter than this. Now, you are in big trouble." Glowering, he told me that he had been watching my slow descent on my makeshift *sari* rope. He then dragged me back inside where the *ma'am* was waiting, a trail of blood following us from the laceration on my leg.

Seething, she glared at me and had me taken to her quarters. Her eyes were narrow and ablaze with fury. She said, "Aasha, you have always been a stupid girl. I don't know what my son sees in you. I warned you, and now you must be punished." As she spoke, she held a spoon over the fire. She watched it until it grew red-hot.

She brought her face inches from mine and spat, "You *must not* forget this day. You *will not* forget this day." As she spoke, she pressed the scorching spoon into my leg, pushing it again and again onto the sensitive skin of my inner thighs. The room grew fuzzy and then went black.

She waited until I returned to consciousness and resumed her spoon-burning punishment. "The next time, you will not be so lucky, Aasha. I will kill you if you try to run again. You belong to me.

Until you repay your debt to me, you cannot leave."

Then, she dismissively sneered, "Let me be honest with you, my dear. Your family doesn't want you back anyway. You are worse than the dust now and have brought great dishonor and shame to them. You are a whore and your body is unclean until you die—there is nothing to run to and no one who will ever, *ever* want you. This is your fate, and there is nothing you can do to change it."

The security guard dragged me down the hallway and dropped me, bleeding, burned, and barely conscious, onto the floor in my cell. In a fog, I wondered and worried, *What if she's right? What if my family won't take me and doesn't want me back?*

For months, I stopped trying to escape, but I often awoke from my sleep with yet another daydream of being home. One day, though, I decided it was time to try again—to give it one last shot to return to my family, hoping that if I made it, they would take me back.

I began to prepare quietly. I watched the comings and goings of the *bosses* and the strong man. This was my last try. My run for freedom had to work. If it didn't, they would kill me.

The morning of my escape, I sat on the roof at sunrise. *This is the day,* I thought. *This is the day I'm going to run for my life.* I felt the already-warm rays of the sun on my skin and listened to the morning bustle on the streets below … rickshaw horns blaring, shopkeepers rolling up the metal doors with a clang, *chaiwallahs* (tea sellers) singing over steaming vats of tea.

Tomorrow, I will not be here. I thought it was a hopeful declaration. The odds were against me, but I would try—I must try. I rose to my feet and headed downstairs, first to the laundry room, and then knocked on my mother-in-law's door.

"We're out of detergent powder, *ma'am.* I'm going to the market to get some. I'll be back in thirty minutes." She studied me for a moment and then drew out some *rupees* for the soap from a drawer in her desk. "Okay, Aasha. Go."

I opened the door. I didn't have shoes, so I walked barefoot toward the market. My heart raced as the spicy aroma of *chiya* stands enveloped me, and the *rupees* grew sweaty in my hand. Arriving at the market, I wound through the stalls, already noisy and bustling with a press of people. *Just what I need to be invisible.* I began to walk faster, looking over my shoulder to see if anyone from the brothel had followed me. Seeing no one, I began to run.

Though still early in the morning, it was already muggy and hot in New Delhi, and sweat dripped into my eyes as I sprinted. The streets swelled with people on foot, bicycles, and auto-rickshaws. Children and adults begged for *rupees*. Street vendors stacked their colorful fruits and vegetables into pyramids on woven mats on the street. Amid it all, I—a fourteen-year-old girl—ran for my life. Bare-foot and breathless, I stopped occasionally to ask, "Which way is it to the railway station please?"

I never stopped running, feeling safely invisible in the little alleys of Paharganj Bazaar, where I saw lots of foreigners in the markets and on the streets. I figured the train station had to be nearby. I was right, for as I turned a corner, I saw the New Delhi Railway Station. Horns blared as rickshaws vied for the business of travelers who arrived in droves to this massive city.

As I got closer, I saw groups of people sitting in the shade of the station, chatting and eating snacks of *parathas* (flat, thick pieces of fried bread) and *chaat* (fried dough topped with potatoes, chickpeas, and yogurt). My hunger didn't slow my steps one beat.

I found the ticket booth. I could not wait my turn—it was way too risky—so I made my way through the line of more than one hundred people, weaving in and out of clusters of families and piles of luggage. I didn't stop when I heard the "tsk, tsk" from someone or when irritated travelers grabbed my arm, trying to stop me from cutting to the front of the line. I pressed on.

Finally, I stood at the ticket window. I took a deep breath and asked the ticket man for help. I knew I didn't have much time—people behind me were tugging at me, trying to push me out of the way.

"Please, sir, please help me. I need a ticket to get home to Nepal." He didn't even look up. He shook his head, "No, no free tickets. No *rupees*? Move out of line!" He looked rushed and stressed and called for the next person in line. A family with a crying baby and five suitcases glared at me and pushed me aside.

I wouldn't give up. I couldn't give up. Surveying the many people around me, I thought, *All I need is one person. Surely there is someone here who will help me.* I began approaching people in the train station, asking them to help me buy a train ticket to get back to Nepal. I begged. I pleaded. I told them snippets of my story.

Finally, one man, eyeing the only thing of value I owned, said *hunchha*. "Yes, I will give you a ticket in exchange for your necklace." My mother-in-law had bought me a white metal necklace, saying it would make me look even more beautiful for the *customers*. I quickly took it off and handed it to the man. In return, he handed me a ticket.

I held the ticket tightly and quickly walked through the press of people toward the train platforms. Each step of the way, I worried that one of the brothel big men or *bosses* would step out of the teeming crowd and grab me. Finally, I found the track that matched the number on my ticket and climbed on the train.

I located an empty seat and curled into a ball, making myself as small and obscure as possible. More people flooded onto the train by the minute, and soon there were people sitting and standing in every square inch of space. Vendors walked outside the window, offering *thalis* (full plates of food), snacks, and *chiya* to go.

The noise of voices from the masses of people in the station outside and inside the train was deafening. But I was grateful for the din, the press of people, and the chaos—and hoped it would keep me safely hidden until the train pulled away.

As the train began to move, I stayed still and didn't speak a word to anyone. Sixteen hours later, after one train transfer in Gorakhpur, I arrived in Kathmandu. I still had a long way to go to make it home.

Still barefoot, I now had nothing. I'd traded my necklace for a train ticket in New Delhi, and my bag, holding the few belongings I had, was stolen on the train.

I found the bus station in Kathmandu and again told my story to strangers, begging for help. One family said yes after the wife tearfully prodded her husband to give me what I needed. I bought my ticket, and I boarded a bus bound for Nepalgunj. We traveled via the Mehendra Highway, Nepal's longest highway and a dusty thoroughfare for travelers bound for the far west of Nepal.

Finally making it to Nepalgunj, I knew I was close to home. I sat down in the shade of a shop to rest for a moment, and a police officer walked by. *This is your chance,* I told myself. So I pulled myself up, walked up to him, and told him my story. "Please, sir, will you help me? I need to get home to my family."

This was risky—I had no papers, and some police officers are as crooked as the brothel *bosses.* But as he listened to me, his eyes softened with kindness, and he bought me a bus ticket. Boarding the bus, I began to relax … just a bit. *After this bus, I will be almost home!*

As the bus dropped me off on the dusty road an hour from my village, I stepped into the cool shade of the jungle and knew just where to go. I headed home on the same path I had walked two years earlier, when Garvesh, the proposal man, had kidnapped me.

As I got closer to home, I became gripped with fear. *Will they accept me? Take me back? Want me? Will my* aama *cry with joy or shame? What will she think when she sees me?*

Emerging out of the jungle, I saw the riverbed and my village perched on its banks. It was midday and hot, so no one was out. I quietly slipped into my home, and I began to cry. Soon, I was weeping. *I made it. I am safe. I am home.* It had taken three days, two trains, and two buses, but I'd finally made it home.

When my mom walked into the house a few hours later, she screamed, thinking there was a stranger in her home. She didn't recognize me. "*Aama*, it's me, Aasha. Mom, I'm home."

Gasping, she took me into her arms, weeping. "Aasha, you're so skinny. I didn't even recognize you. Where have you been?"

I hid my face, ashamed of how I looked and worried at what she would say next. She brushed the tears from my cheeks and held me close. Then she took a breath, stood up, and began to warm some milk for *chiya*.

As she stood over the stove, she spoke, "When you went into the jungle and never returned, we notified the police. For weeks, we looked for you. We thought you were eaten by a wild animal. I cried for days, sure that you were dead."

I spent the next few days in the house, terrified to leave. I slept, ate, and told my family the story of Garvesh and my barefoot escape. Three days later, one of the brothel's strongmen showed up in our village, looking for me. He pounded on our door, demanding that *their property* be returned. My brave *buba* said, "No! You cannot have my *chhori* back. We know how many girls you've already taken. We filed a report with the police, and they are on our side."

As he turned on his heels and walked away from our hut, the brothel big man shouted one last threat, "Aasha, we'll be back. You'll never be safe!"

Over and over, my dad risked everything to protect us, to stand up for his daughters. That day, my brave *buba* was the biggest man in my eyes.

Chosen by the Maoists (2005)

After I'd been home a few months, the Maoists returned to our village. During the ongoing conflict, the police often required our help. One night, it was past midnight. Most of our village was asleep. The police pounded on the doors of our huts, waking us up, demanding that the children step outside. As they scanned the crowd of sleepy kids, many of us hid behind our parents. I saw the eyes of the police chief land on me.

"You, girl, come here. You look clever. How old are you?"

"Fourteen," I whispered.

"You must come with us."

My *buba* said, "No, please, sir, no! This is my daughter. She's been through so much—too much—already. Please don't take her. Please, I beg you. Take me instead."

But the chief and the other officers didn't seem to listen. They led me away. One of the policemen held my arm with one hand and his gun with his other hand. I had no choice but to go where I was told.

My family and many of the villagers followed us up the hill that led from our village to the main road above. Approaching the chief, my father asked what it was they needed me to do. "It's not your business, old man. Stop bothering us. Be quiet." My dad lowered his head and stopped talking. But he stayed close to us.

Our steps were lit by the light of a full moon. As I walked with the team of policemen, I heard the familiar voices of my parents, sisters, and our neighbors speaking softly to each other and the gentle pounding of their many feet trailing us on the winding dirt road. After walking a bit further, the officers drew us to a stop. They pointed to a tree that blocked the road ahead, and they were hesitant to get much closer. I wondered what made these big policemen nervous. They told me, "You, clever little girl—we need you to go to that tree and collect the doll that is in its branches."

I didn't understand. *A doll? Why did they wake me up in the middle of the night to get a doll from a tree, and why were they so nervous?* I trembled slightly, as I wondered why they seemed so uneasy and why they needed me to get the doll from the fallen tree's branches in the dark of the night.

The police chief continued, "The Maoists have blocked the road and have planted a bomb in that doll in the tree. We have some supplies we need to get through tonight. You will climb into the branches, collect the doll-bomb, and carry it away from the tree so that we can move it tonight. Go now, little girl. We need you to act quickly." One of the officers pushed me with his gun barrel.

My *buba* broke his silence, desperately protesting. He begged the chief, "Please, no, please no. She will die. My daughter will die if you force her to do this."

They didn't even turn to look at him. They just sneered at each other and pushed me ahead. "Old man, you *Badi* are the dust. What does it matter if one of your girls dies? You sell your own girls all the time, anyway, so don't talk to us about protecting your precious daughter."

I did as they said and began to walk, my heart beating thunderously through my chest. As I approached the tree with the doll-bomb in its branches, I stepped up gently onto the fallen tree and surveyed the spot where the doll had been placed on one of the branches. *You can do this, Aasha*, I told myself. I took a breath and climbed, remembering that my sisters nicknamed me *bandar* for my monkey climbing skills. Whenever a branch snapped, I could hear the villagers gasp.

Reaching the doll, I took hold of it in one hand and used the other to balance myself, throwing the doll with all my might into the jungle. The explosion's thunder could be heard for miles, and it lit up the sky with a bright burst. Branches and rocks were hurled into the air, but no one was injured. Some ran away as I hurled the doll; others crouched behind tree stumps. I wasn't surprised because we've been running and hiding for a long time. Our lives have depended on it.

A Dream Turns into a Nightmare (2013)

After all that had happened to me during my days on G.B. Road, I had become fixed in my determination to never be with a man again … never to fall in love … and never to marry. But when I was fifteen, I fell in love. Bishal was a boy I'd grown up with in our village, and he was kind to me. My parents had always liked him and said he was "a good boy." In Nepal, most marriages are arranged, but some couples choose to marry for love. That was Bishal and me. We fell in love, went to India to find work, and got married.

I never expected to return to India. But with Bishal, I would go anywhere. And work was hard to come by in Nepal. So, we began our lives together in India. When I was eighteen, I gave birth to Preeti, a beautiful *chhori*, and two years later, to Suraj, a *chhora*. How I loved these two little ones! Each new day arrived on my doorstep like a sweet gift of love and life from the hands of God, just for me.

While we lived in India, I stayed connected with my family. I wanted to make sure they knew I was safe and happy and that our family was growing. One day, Hannah called to share her next big idea with me: "Aasha, *didi*, how about you send Preeti to Kathmandu so she can go to school? Not only is this a very good opportunity for her, but she'll be with her family ... her cousins *and* me! I think *this* is the best way to create a good future for her! What do you think?" I talked with my husband about it, and a few months later, when Preeti was almost four years old, we decided it *was* a very good idea indeed. I took her to Kathmandu, introduced her to Auntie Hannah and her cousins, got her settled in her dormitory with her new family of friends, and then went home to visit my parents in our village.

When I returned to our village of Jhuprakhola, I saw three other women who were also visiting, on holiday. They were friends of mine from childhood, and they had each found jobs in Kuwait as housekeepers. As we do in our village, we spent time sitting over *chiya* and talking. During our *chiya* talks, they told me about how well their employers treated them, how much money they were making, and how happy they were. They told me that there was a man in our village—they called him "a broker"—who helped them find a family-employer in need of a housekeeper. They suggested that I talk to him and see if he could help me too. I tracked him down and asked if he knew of any other families in need of a housekeeper.

"Ah, you're in luck, Aasha!" He was excited and told me that he had a list of families looking for help. "It will be easy to arrange. It's up to you to decide how soon you want to start." The broker told me I could go anytime and that he would take care of my flight, work visa, and paperwork. When he told me how much I could make as a housekeeper, I was shocked. It was twice as much as I was able to make at my job in India! By my calculations, I could make enough money in two years of work in Kuwait to be able to move back to Nepal and live, together, as a family. I told him I would call him after I returned to India and talked with my husband.

The next week, I went back to India. I was so happy to see my husband and son. I'd missed them so much. But my heart ached for my daughter too. It didn't feel good to be separated from her, even though I was happy she was going to school and living with her cousins and Aunt Hannah.

As I talked with Bishal, we decided it was a good opportunity to make more money for our family with this housekeeping job in Kuwait. If we were able to save enough, we could move back to Nepal to live together as a family. I called the broker in our village and told him I was ready. In just a few weeks, he had everything arranged, and it was time for me to leave.

I was very sad to say goodbye to my son and husband but also extremely excited at the prospect that our family would be reunited and financially more secure. Two years of separation was worth it. I was determined to be strong, work hard, and focus each day on the goal of living reunited with my family.

When I landed in Kuwait, my excitement was quickly extinguished. Within days, my dreams and determination turned into a nightmare. The family who had hired me was very, very cruel, and immediately began to beat me. They treated me terribly. The man of the house forced me to have sex with him and to massage and touch his private parts.

I wished I had never come, but I had no way to get home. I did not speak the language and had no way to report the abuse. I was not able to leave until my contract was up in two years. I was trapped. Enslaved, once again.

Each day, I tried not to focus on the pain and struggle and instead counted down the days until I could go home and be with my family again.

Amid the nightmare, one day, hope dawned. I was in the market and heard my language. *Someone is speaking Nepali!* I walked around the market to see who it was. Finding two women chattering away in *Nepali*, I walked up to them and, after greeting them with our customary, "*Namaste,*" I blurted out my story. It was risky, but I was desperate, so I told them everything.

I told them about my family and the beatings in my household in Kuwait. I spoke briefly of my days on G.B. Road. I begged them to help me. "I want to go home and be with my husband and children. Is there anything you can do to help me? I don't know if I will ever again have the chance to talk with anyone else from Nepal." I pleaded and waited for their response. The women looked at each other as I held my breath.

Looking back at me, they nodded, and one said briskly, "Come with us." As we made our way out of the market and into their car, they talked to each other and came up with a plan. They took me straight to the Embassy of Nepal. I stayed in a safe house in Nepal's embassy in Kuwait with three hundred other women from my country as the officials sorted out my case. I was given the job to cook for the women in the safe house, and as I did, I heard their stories. Just like me, most of them had come to Kuwait for work, with the promise of making money and with dreams of a better future. And, just like me, the promises proved to be false. Life in Kuwait was a far cry from a dream come true. I remember talking with some women who inspired me, planting seeds of hope and faith that I would be all right and that God was with me and loved me.

Many of these women had been waiting in the embassy's safe

house for years and would, most likely, never be able to leave. I heard that some had died while waiting for their passports and paperwork that were required for them to return home to Nepal. But I was *a lucky one.* In four months, my family sent me my passport, and the embassy gave me permission and the needed documentation to return home. I was so thankful and very excited!

When I landed in Kathmandu, my sister Hannah was there to greet me. "Aasha, *didi,* welcome home! Sister, we have been praying for you and never lost hope that this moment—your return to us—would happen!" She told me that my husband and son were on their way from India, and my daughter was excitedly waiting for me. She had secured a job for me—and my husband—at the school where our daughter attended. We could stay in Nepal, *and* we each had jobs. "Aasha sister, my dear *didi,* you have had enough heartache for one lifetime. Please stay here with us."

I took the hand of my brave *bahini*—my brave little sister Hannah—and nodded. "Yes, I'll stay."

No Longer Landless (2018)

Today, as I sit and reflect on these stories and on my life, I am in awe. I am grateful. I can barely believe it. My husband and I love our work for the school. Our children are happy and thriving. We are together, as a family, which is truly a dream come true. He is a bus driver, and I do all kinds of jobs—take care of school children, clean, make *chiya.* Whatever they need me to do, I do.

And yet, even after we were married, the *ma'am* and her bodyguards still threatened me. We paid thousands upon thousands of *rupees* to the *ma'am* to pay off my "debt." We wanted to demonstrate to her that we would not back down and that she no longer had any power over me, nor did she own me. Thankfully, she stopped harassing us and has left us alone.

I am now free and do not belong to her.

We worked very hard for many years. We saved every *rupee*—all our money—and in 2018, we made history and bought a piece of land in Kathmandu. I know of no other *Badi* who bought land before us, and if that is true, then that made us the first of our landless people to own land in the capital of our nation. This was no small thing, and we were grateful and in awe that our dreams were coming true!

But we will not stop working toward our next dream. Now, we are saving for a house. It will likely be the first house built by a *Badi* in Kathmandu. I expect it will take us many more years to save the money we need to build it, but we have done harder things. Together, we will get it done.

Sakhira: The Fighter

Fleeing a Bad Man (2007)

I was born in a *Badi* village in the far west of Nepal in 1996. My dad didn't like to work. He was very unkind to my mom, badly and regularly abusing my *aama*. Ruthlessly, he beat my mom with his hands *and* beat her down with his words.

When I was ten years old, she decided that life with my dad was far too uncertain and unsafe. Wanting more for her children, she gathered us up and ran away. It was very risky, but she was determined. We moved to Jhuprakhola, a *Badi* village near a river that was surrounded by jungle.

We lived near Hannah, and as we became friends, she told me about Puja and Gita and her sisters Aasha and Meena, who had—one by one—disappeared in the jungle years ago. Our new village neighbors agreed and warned me to be careful, saying, "Girls go missing from here all the time."

As we got settled in the village, my mom met a man, and they soon married. At first, it seemed that my stepdad would treat us better than my dad did. But it was not to be. He was an alcoholic, and he drank a lot of homemade liquor called *rakshi*. One day, he left the village, never to return. I haven't seen him since.

My family continued to struggle to make a living. There was not much work for anyone. What little work there was didn't pay much, so many villagers were forced to leave the country for work. When my *aama* decided that she, too, needed to go to India in search of a job, she left me in the care of my big sister and her husband.

My *didi* left each morning to carry stones from the riverbed to the road. (This was common work for women in our village.) She was paid only a few *rupees* at the end of her dusty and grueling day's work. But life at home for me, while she was away each day, was worse. The moment she left, it was just her husband and me. Although I didn't like how he teased and mocked me, I really hated how he looked at me. It made my skin crawl.

One day, he offered me a drink, and it made my head dizzy. As I stumbled outside to get some fresh air, he grabbed me and pulled me toward him. Smashed up against him, I could smell his alcohol breath. His eyes were wild and aggressive.

I am a fighter. Always have been, always will be. I hit him, bit him, and pushed him off me. He was stronger than me, but luckily for me, he moved slowly because he'd been drinking. As I ran for the door, he glared and spat his threat, "If you tell your sister or anyone in this village, Sakhira, I will tell them that *you* flirted with *me*. No one will believe you, a bad and seductive eleven-year-old girl."

What to do? I knew he was right. The next morning, I ran away.

I couldn't tell my sister, and I wouldn't stay one more day in the house with him. There had to be a better life, a better way to live than *this*.

Dangerous and Drugged Chiya (2007)

I walked all day, and as the night grew dark, I stopped at a guesthouse in Chinchu, a town not too far from my village, and asked the owner if I could do some work in exchange for a place to stay that night. He said yes, and when he saw that I was a good worker, he allowed me to stay longer and help in the kitchen. But when the other cooks and servers in the kitchen heard I was *Badi*, they began touching me and speaking to me badly. In the middle of the night, I ran from the guesthouse and journeyed on to Surkhet.

Once in Surkhet, I wandered and slept on the streets for fifteen days. When I grew hungry, I dug for food in trash cans. I finally found work as a dishwasher at a restaurant. One day, I was happy to see a familiar face, as my cousin and a friend of hers entered the restaurant.

They waited for me to step outside after work, and when I did, they asked me to take a walk with them. My cousin spoke first, "Sakhira, this is no place for you. You are all alone and working too hard for not enough money. Come with us—we're going shopping in Nepalgunj tomorrow, and we'll buy you some nice clothes. It's several hours from here by bus, but it is a nice place. Do you want to come with us?" It sounded good to me, so the next morning, my cousin, her friend Rita, and I made our way to the border town of Nepalgunj, where four men met us.

My stomach was upset from the long day of travel, and when I saw the men, it churned even more. I was scared. Something about them did not seem quite right. My cousin came to my side, saying, "Sakhira, you look worried. Let's go get some *chiya*. I also have some medicine that will help your stomach."

As we sat at the roadside tea stand and sipped our *chiya*, she gave me the stomach medicine and talked kindly to me. I began to relax and became so sleepy that I fell out of my chair. The world went black.

When I woke up, I had no idea where I was. My cousin heard me waking up and came into the room, saying, "Sakhira, that medicine for your stomach must have made you tired. When you fell asleep at the *chiya* stand, we brought you here, to Rita's house. Why don't you take a shower? I'll bring you some breakfast." As she started the shower for me, she kept chatting, "Isn't this home nice? You're so lucky because Rita's family has offered you a job to take care of their children. They are rich, and they will pay you well!"

I took a shower, which felt nice. After she brought me food, I devoured every morsel on my plate. I didn't realize how hungry I was! Then I fell asleep again, and I never saw my cousin or Rita again.

Sold to a Brothel (2007)

The next day, I was instructed to go to the market to get some groceries for dinner. A rickshaw pulled up to the house, and as I got in, I found that there were two girls sitting in it already. As the rickshaw wove us through a marketplace of restaurants, shops, and *chiya* stands, the girls began talking.

"Sakhira, when your cousin and her friend sold you, they made a lot of money. You now belong to a family who lives on G.B. Road, one of India's red-light districts. It is where you, too, will live. But don't worry. If you work hard and make enough money, you can go home again."

Sitting inside that rickshaw, my mind reeled. *My cousin sold me, and I belong to a family? What does that even mean? What work am I going to do, and how will I be able to make enough money to go home?*

Soon, I began to see girls standing in doorways, looking very beautiful. Their lips were painted bright red, and there were men of all kinds—some looked poor, others rich—walking, eating, drinking, and *looking.*

The rickshaw stopped in front of a trio of clothing shops. Some girls in the floors above leaned out of the windows to gaze at the street below. Other windows were barred, and in the dark rooms behind, I could see faint movement.

I had chills of foreboding and fear.

Just then, a strong-looking man came out of the shop and took my arm firmly. His eyes were dark and aggressive. My muscles tightened in apprehension. Pushing me up a dark stairway at the back of the shop, he forcefully pressed his hand into my back to make sure we moved quickly.

I didn't know what to do, but I had to do something. I began to yell, scratching and punching him as he dragged me down the hallway. It didn't slow him down at all, but he grew annoyed. He covered my mouth and told me to be quiet. I kept shouting at the top of my lungs and told him, "No, I will not be quiet." I did not want to be there and would not do whatever *work* this place required. I determined to find someplace else to go.

The big man shoved me into a room at the end of a hallway, where a woman awaited us. She glowered at me with a cruel gaze. I feared her even more than I did the big man. She stared at me, her eyes rolling up and down over me—over all of me. I squirmed, terribly uncomfortable at her blatant examination of me. As she began to speak, her words were authoritative and steeped in contempt. "Sakhira, I own you. You belong to me until you repay the price I paid for you. You cannot leave until you do. You will begin working for me tonight. Men come here for pleasure, for companionship, for sex. You will do whatever they ask."

"No, never!" I shouted. Immediately, the *boss* shouted, and the strong man appeared. He took me into a small concrete room and beat me. Beat me hard. Each blow drove home that *this* was the sort of power that ruled *this* place.

I dropped to the ground, and he leaned in close with a savage whisper, "Your voice, loud as it may be, will not save you here. I don't know how it was in your village, but here, your fighting will not save you—it will hurt you. If you are smart, you'll do as she says. She is the *boss*—the *ma'am*—of this place."

A different woman entered the room and began to stir a powdery-looking substance into a bottle of beer. She forced my mouth open and poured it down my throat. The world went fuzzy, then black. I entertained my first *customers* that night, although I don't remember much. I was barely conscious, but I still felt it—the searing pain and the sense of utter incapacity to stop it, to stop them.

For a week, I was locked in a cell, my mind hazy and dazed in fog. Men came and went, using and abusing me as they wished. There were so many that I lost count. They smelled like sex, sweat, and alcohol. I began to take on the same smells. I started to think, *Even though I'm just eleven, I bet I will die here. This is my fate—what can I do to change it?*

After a few weeks, they moved me out of the cell and into a barred room. In the press of thirty other girls and women, I soon learned that Hannah's sister Meena and friends Gita and Puja were in this brothel too. I began to look for them, and when I found them, we tried to find a few moments to share our stories of how we each got there. We had to be quick and sneaky because the guards didn't allow us to talk with each other. When they found us whispering to each other, we received more than a few fierce tongue-lashings and beatings.

Meena, Gita, and Puja told me that there were at least fifty girls from other *Badi* villages in this brothel. I told Meena that her family thought she'd been eaten by a wild animal in the jungle and that Hannah missed her so much.

Over the coming weeks and months, our conversations slowed and finally stopped. *What more was there to talk about?* Besides, we were tired of being beaten.

They beat us into submission … and into isolation.

The darkness and dreariness of the place, with its dank and dirty smells, slowly became familiar. I believed they were now part of my life. I spoke to no one. I slept whenever I could to make the days go by faster.

The brothel had a tiny restaurant on the first floor. Some days, when I had a few *rupees* of my own, I was able to buy food for myself. I was given *rupees* of my own only if the *boss* was pleased with how much money I had brought in the night before. If she wasn't pleased, she gave me nothing, and I had no money to buy food. I was hungry all the time.

As my hunger and desperation grew, I tried to run away four times. It never worked. The *boss* had the strong man of the brothel watching for runners day and night. Every time I tried to run, I was always found, brought back, and punished with beatings, followed by drugs and alcohol that were forcibly poured down my throat. Sometimes, I was kept in a dark cell alone and given the most violent men for *customers* at night.

Nakedness and sex were everywhere and constant. There were no windows in the cell where I stayed. I could not see outside. All I saw were girls and men. Beer bottles lined the floor, punctuated by puddles of brick-red *paan*.

No one treated me with kindness. Not ever. No one seemed trustworthy or good. I was surrounded by many, and yet, I was alone. I sat and stared at the walls. There were girls everywhere, but friendship did not exist. It wasn't allowed. We were too busy anyway—either busy *working* or sleeping.

Every day was a nightmare. I believed I was living in the pit of hell and began to live each day with less hope than the day before. I stopped crying, stopped screaming, stopped punching.

Sakhira *the fighter* stopped fighting.

Electrocuted by the Police (2009)

Brothels in India and the police have a complex relationship. I was told that it was illegal for brothels to "employ" young girls. Though illegal, I saw it every day: *child prostitution* was lucrative and brought more *customers* ... which was the name of the game on G.B. Road.

The first time I saw the police officers come through our brothel on a raid, I recognized a few of them as our most regular *customers*. I'd also heard that they received bribes frequently from the *ma'am*.

They were paid to look the other way. I even saw her pay them once, and I didn't trust them, thinking, *They are not here to save us, that's for sure. It is all for show.*

But sometimes the police were pressured by news agencies or NGOs, or for political reasons, to crack down on child prostitution and trafficking. They would "raid" our brothel, but nothing much happened when they did. The *ma'am* was more powerful.

On one such day, an NGO tipped the police that there were underage girls in our brothel. At that time, many of us were under the age of eighteen. I'd been in the brothel for nearly two years and was now thirteen years old. Several girls were under the age of ten— the youngest was seven. We did as we were told and quietly scrambled into the small closet where the youngest girls were forced to hide during a raid.

An older girl told me later that as the police quickly walked through the many rooms of our brothel and methodically scanned the faces of the 250 women, it seemed as though they had been told about the closet where we were hiding.

As the door to our closet opened, we saw them. The police officers feigned surprise, and NGO officials seemed extremely excited to have found us. They led the youngest twelve of us out the brothel's door and into a truck that was waiting for us in the street below. They drove us to the police station. Under the watchful eyes of the NGO officials, the police gave us food and water. The NGO took pictures of each of us and said they would send them off for publication in Indian and Nepali newspapers with the headline, "Found Girls in a G.B. Road Brothel." They hoped our families would see the pictures and come for us.

A few hours later, once the officials were gone, the brothel owner showed up. We heard her shouting at the police to return us to her immediately. "We have an agreement. Don't forgo your end of our bargain. You'll regret it."

The officers explained that the officials were watching them. "They are coming back tomorrow. They already took pictures and are posting them in newspapers in India and Nepal. Right now, they are more powerful even than you, *ma'am*. We cannot do as you ask this time."

I was in the police station for twenty-five days. The NGO officials came from time to time to check on us. They told us they had received some phone calls from family members who saw pictures of us in their papers.

It might seem that being in police custody would be a safe place to be, but it was not. Far from it. Whenever the NGO staff was present, the police treated us relatively well. But the moment the NGO officials left, they forced us to drink their urine and laughed uproariously as we did. When they heard I was a *Badi*, it got even worse. They began calling me a whore, an animal, and garbage. They touched me whenever and wherever they wanted. My days began to be just like those I'd spent in the brothel … maybe even worse.

The fighter in me rose again. I spit out the urine into their faces, yelled back at them, and clawed at them when they tried to touch me. I told them I would report their treatment of me to the officials. Perhaps they grew scared. They hid me in the psychiatric section of the jail, far away from the eyes of the monitoring NGO officials.

The brothel owner heard about my fighting and screaming, and she must have grown worried about what I might reveal if I were released. I heard that she bribed the police to shut me up.

Then the nightmare worsened.

For several days, the police repeatedly put me in a bathtub filled with cold water and attached probes to my forehead. They sent electric shocks through my brain and body. I heard them talking to each other about "trying to scramble … scatter … eradicate memories." I fell into a stupor and don't recall much from those days.

Back in Nepal, my sister happened to see my photo in the newspaper. She and my mom had been looking for me for two years. My sister called my mom, ecstatic, "She's alive, *Aama*! Sakhira is alive and in New Delhi at the police station." The next morning, my sister set out for New Delhi. She arrived at the police station a few days later with the newspaper in hand and demanded to see me.

As she entered my cell, she found her *bahini* was broken. She later told me that she didn't even recognize me as I lay there unconscious and malnourished, barely alive. The police were forced to let me go, and slowly, we made our way back to Nepal.

When I first got back to my village, my brain was foggy. I don't remember much about my first month back home. Even though the days were hot, and inside my sister's hut, it was hotter yet, I didn't go outside. I didn't eat or drink much. I slept all day and zoned out. My sister came to visit me as often as she could, and I saw that she was worried.

Desperate, she decided to try to track down Hannah, who had just left for Kathmandu the previous month with thirty-three other girls from our village. Hannah's parents had a phone number that had been given to them if they needed to get in touch with her. My sister called the number the next morning and asked if she could talk with Hannah. Tearfully, she told Hannah everything and begged for her to do what she could to help me get to Kathmandu too. "She's not doing well here. I don't know how to help her. Please, Hannah, see what you can do."

Hannah assured my sister that she'd do what she could. A few days later, Raju arrived. Although he'd been to the village many times before, this was my first chance to meet him. Raju came to my house and asked me directly, "Sakhira, do you want to live in Kathmandu and go to school? I know you've had a very difficult few years. It's probably not easy to trust people right now." As he spoke, I saw tears in his eyes.

He told me that he, too, was a *Dalit*—an *untouchable*. He said he knew what it was like to be judged and to be treated unjustly. He continued, "Sakhira, it's your choice. Do you want to come?"

I didn't expect that he'd live up to his promises, but I said yes. I thought, *Why not? Even if the promises are only a little true, my life will be better than it is now.*

As we traveled to Kathmandu, we talked a little, and I slept a lot. He told me that his sister and a few others would work with me and support whatever I needed to help me heal from the trauma of the last two years.

In Kathmandu, I met the other girls in my dormitory. Right away, I felt something I had never felt before: hope. These people lived lives of love. They really seemed to care for me. Each day, they reminded me that I was loved, that healing was possible, and that *this* was a new beginning.

I sat over *chiya* with other girls who told me about their stories of abduction, false promises, drugs, and abuse. Their stories were like mine. But I was not sure that I could ever be free—be happy—like them. *Could my tiny bit of hope ever grow into the big hope they hold?* The whispers of shame in my head were persistent and strong. *You will never be strong and brave like them. Never. You're broken. Beyond repair.*

Learning how to live free was not easy. Although I no longer lived in the brothel, it had left its mark on me. Some days, my body longed for sex. Other days, for drugs. And others, for alcohol. It didn't make sense—these were the very things that had almost killed me. My eyes grew shadowed and angry. *Had the brothel days ruined me?*

There I was, living with a future that glittered with possibility, but I was shackled by the past. I slunk into the depths of despair.

Even more troubling was that little by little, over time, the memories began to trickle back from my two years in New Delhi. I had flashbacks of the brothel—the beatings, the hunger, the thousands of men, the rescue, the electrocution, the police. The scars on my forehead reminded me. I rubbed my fingers over them, thinking, *I'm damaged goods. No one will ever want me again. The scars on my forehead are ugly—and so am I.*

My sister, Hannah, and many of her trusted friends told me that I could be healed, that good could grow out of this pain, but how? When?

Happily Ever After (2016)

Bistarai, slowly, I developed friendships that strengthened me. It didn't happen quickly, but as days turned into weeks, months, and years, I felt better and more hopeful. I did my best in school, and when I neared the end of that year's studies, I decided to go back to my village. I wanted to be home and be with my family.

I first went to my village of Jhuprakhola, but I didn't stay there long. I'd heard that my sister had gone to India to take care of our *aama*, who was still working in India, so I decided to go to India to see them both. I had not seen them since I was eleven, before I'd run away from my brother-in-law for Surkhet. I missed them and decided it was time.

I never expected to fall in love in India, but I fell hard the moment I met Mahesh. He was such a good man, a man I never thought I would deserve to love or be loved by. From the beginning, I decided to keep nothing from him. I told him everything. This was a big risk—I feared that the moment he heard my story, he would run the other way. But he didn't run. He looked at me with tenderness after hearing my whole story. He said, "Sakhira, I'll be your husband to you today, not the husband to your past." We got married when I was twenty years old.

Ever since we met, I told him about my friends and family in Kathmandu, so after we were married for one year, he suggested that we return to Nepal. He said, "You can finish your schooling and see your friends. I really want to meet them."

So, that's what we did. We returned to Kathmandu.

Today, I'm happy … so very happy. First, I will finish my studies and graduate from high school. After that, I have three big dreams: to go to university and study humanities, rescue girls who are trapped in brothels, and own a home in Kathmandu with my husband. For now, each day, I am grateful to be with the love of my life and back with my family and friends, where I am loved and where I belong.

Hannah (Part Two): 5 Rescues.
3 Preventions. 5 Years.

My Best Friends, Puja and Gita (2011)
1st Rescue Team: Raju and Hannah

After six years of living with headaches, muscle pain, and fainting spells, I'd found a way to get by with the pain. I thought that would be the story of my life. But by the end of my first year living in Kathmandu, I was ecstatic to find that my symptoms were completely gone. It's true—*satya*. They were gone, and I was grateful each day. My fears and anxieties lessened. I even found myself relaxing a little. For the first time ever, I began to look forward to my future.

School was even more wonderful than I imagined it would be. I loved it. I devoured every word that came from my teachers' mouths, read every book available, and studied as hard as I could. I felt I needed to make up for lost time. When I did take a break, it was most often to sing and dance with my friends or—a real treat!—to watch a *Bollywood* movie together. They told me they'd never seen me smiling so much (I'd noticed the same when I saw them). I loved spending time with my niece, Bina (Meena's daughter). I felt protective of her, and I constantly kept my eyes on her to make sure she was safe and doing well. What I saw delighted me. She was thriving, both with her friends and in school, and that was no less than a miracle.

I, too, was flourishing. There was plenty of food, a community of support, and security. In fact, my friends and I talked often about how it didn't even cross our minds anymore that a man might climb through our windows at night to try and have sex. Back in the village, it was a possibility every single night.

One day after school, my phone rang, and I heard the voices that I'd been dreaming to hear for the past seven years. I squealed—maybe even screamed—with joy. It was Puja and Gita, my two best friends from the village who'd gone missing when I was eight. I couldn't believe it! They were alive and back in our village!

We chattered, speaking a mile a minute, sharing stories of the seven years since we were last together in our village. As they talked, I was struck by how very different our lives had been since we were last together. They confirmed what I had heard: Gita and Puja's cousin was a pimp and had sold them to a brothel on G.B. Road.

They told me that they were home for a few weeks for a festival. "The *ma'am* is confident that we will return to the brothel because she has a lot of family in the village watching us. As further assurance, she sent a security guard to keep an eye on us to 'Make sure we don't get any big ideas and run away.'"

I burst out and asked, "How about you come here to Kathmandu and go to school, stay in the dormitories, and live with me? Sisters, what kind of life is it for you in the brothel? What kind of future do you have there?" They were quiet and said they'd think about it.

I was confused. Why the hesitation? Why the delay? Life on G.B. Road was terrible. If they came to Kathmandu, they had an opportunity of a lifetime waiting for them. (I had a lot to learn about how complex this choice was for those surrounded by the insidious darkness and oppression of life in a brothel.) I tried to convince them to not delay, but Gita cut me off. "Hannah, wait—before we talk anymore, I have something to tell you. It's very important. Your sister

Meena is alive."

I stood in stunned silence. *Meena is alive?*

Puja jumped in with more information. "When she went missing, she was sold to a brothel on G.B. Road by Chaha. For years, we were at the same brothel on G.B. Road. A few years ago, she was moved to Meerut, a place for older brothel workers. And, Hannah, she has two beautiful little girls—you have two more nieces!"

My mind began racing, and then it snapped back into focus. "Okay, sisters, please make sure you tell my *aama* what you've told me. My mom has been to Delhi more times than I can count over the past few years to look for Meena. I know she'll want to go back once she has a better idea of where she is located and hears about Meena's baby girls."

I heard a man's voice shouting in the background, and suddenly the line went dead. I stood, dumbfounded, looking at the phone. What to do? I wanted, with everything in me, to go to India at that very moment to find my sister and my nieces. I had some finals coming up for school and knew I couldn't go with my mom just then, but I worried for my mom's safety if she went again alone. To do so was a dangerous endeavor.

I began to feel frantic, short of breath, and more than a little distraught. But I took a breath and closed my eyes. I began to pray. As I did, my heart's racing slowed a bit and so did the freight train of my mind. I knew that what would be required was more than I could accomplish alone. It would take a miracle to get my sister and nieces, along with Puja and Gita, safely home and free of G.B. Road's unjust grip—but I was not going to give up until they were all safely home in Nepal.

My mom called me the next day. She had talked with Gita and Puja in the village, and as I expected, she was determined to try again to find Meena and her girls. I was incredulous and asked her, "*Aama,* you have two granddaughters! Can you believe it?"

She was quiet for a minute, and then said, "No, I cannot—and yet, I had a feeling that Meena was still alive. Imagining her baby girls makes me want to leave right now! Let me just say this, Hannah my love, I'm not stopping until your sister and her children are back home in Nepal with us." I smiled, remembering that I'd had that same thought the previous day. Like mother, like daughter, I guess.

She left the next week to try again to find Meena, hopeful that with the information my friends had given her, she'd finally have success. Meerut, where my friends said Meena was living, was not just chaotic and challenging to navigate but was as unsafe as G.B. Road. She returned two weeks later, disappointed. Try as she might, she was unable to find the place where Meena was living.

When I turned sixteen years old, I began to travel to different parts of Nepal, to Singapore, Australia, and Sweden. Interest was growing and people wanted to learn about human trafficking and our *Badi* people. Some wanted to give money; others wanted to become more informed, active, or connected to our organization.

What an unbelievable change two years had made in my life! Never in my wildest dreams did I think I'd be in school, traveling internationally, and speaking to large groups about my people's story. I was often split between two thoughts: *Pinch me! I am so grateful for all these incredible opportunities,* and, *There is so much left to do to make a dent in this big problem that is impacting so many of those I love!* I couldn't imagine the struggles my sister Meena and her daughters must be facing each day. Gita and Puja were also often on my mind, and I wondered how they were doing.

One day, while in Sweden, my phone rang, and I heard the breathless voices of Puja and Gita. Gita spoke first, "Hannah, we are back in the village, and the bodyguard is with us again. We aren't supposed to make unaccompanied phone calls. Sister, we need to make this fast."

Puja jumped in, "Hannah, can we still come to Kathmandu to live with you and go to school? We are back in our village, Jhuprak-hola, for two weeks. We'd like to come soon but need to be careful. The *ma'am* sent a bodyguard again."

I told them that I would ask Raju Uncle to come for them within a few days.

After our call the previous year, I had immediately told Raju about Puja and Gita. He had given me his word that if my friends decided they wanted to come, he would do whatever he could to bring them to Kathmandu.

The timing was now perfect. We had just opened our first halfway house for rescued girls, with a focused and supportive environment for some of the needs they had as survivors—after being serially raped, addicted to drugs, and suffering from post-traumatic stress. It had been eight years since Gita and Puja were first trafficked to New Delhi. I was sure they were going to need a lot of support when they arrived.

The moment I got off the phone, I immediately called Raju and asked him if he could go right away to the village to rescue my friends. He did as I asked and as he had promised, taking the twenty-hour bus ride from Kathmandu to my village. He found the girls and, with them, the bodyguard.

At this point, Raju had become a familiar sight to our villagers. First, he did as he always did when he came to visit. He sipped *chiya* and talked to my family and our neighbors about how they were doing, and he shared stories about how their girls were faring in their studies and travels. As he did so, he looked for an occasion to talk with Gita and Puja privately.

One afternoon, as the village was busy and abuzz with preparing for a festival feast, Raju noticed that the bodyguard was not with Puja and Gita. Seizing the opportunity, Raju approached them, gave them my greetings, and made sure they knew who he was. He asked them if it was true that they wanted to leave the brothel and come to Kathmandu to live and go to school. They told him *ho*. Although they were nervous, yes, they were sure. They did not want to return to the brothel on G.B. Road.

That night, Raju spoke with Puja and Gita's parents, and with their permission, the three quickly and quietly left the village. Raju had instructed a neighbor to share a message with the bodyguard and brothel *boss*. "These girls have made their choice. Because we want no trouble with you, I promise to pay you every month for two more years until their purchase price is repaid and to more than cover the loss of income you'll have." (In order to protect my friends and ensure their freedom, Raju was true to his word and sent money each month for two years until their purchase price was fully repaid.)

When I returned from Sweden and saw my best friends sitting in our dormitory, I flung my arms around each of them in tearful wonder. I couldn't believe it! They were here, and they were safe, standing right in front of me. I pledged, "I'll do whatever I can to help you, I promise. We are sister-friends forever!"

I stayed with them for a week in our new halfway house. On the first night, just before she went to sleep, Puja whispered, "Hannah sister, I'll do whatever I can to help you, I promise. I think if I go with you, we can find Meena."

I put my arm around her and gave her a squeeze, saying, "This is quite an offer. You are so brave, Puja."

But first, I knew that Puja needed time to heal and to learn how to live in this new life of school and community. I had experienced it myself and seen it over and over: Often, learning to embrace a life of freedom was not easy. Some days, it was like watching birds with battered and broken wings trying to fly.

It would take Gita and Puja a while to become accustomed to their new life of freedom, but together and *bistarai*, we would slowly make our way.

Meena's Daughters (2012)
2nd Rescue Team: Aama Maya, Puja, and Bahadur

Puja was eager to go back to New Delhi with my mom to help bring back Meena and her girls. I was again in Sweden speaking about human trafficking. We put together a small rescue team of my mom, Puja, and a kind and strong man named Bahadur.

We depended a lot on Gita and Puja for the rescue strategy, and we decided to go with their recommendation that we go in first to get Meena's girls, Nanu and Kaya, and then return for my sister later. Having been at the brothel when both of Meena's daughters were taken from their mom and moved to G.B. Road and that Meena was still being housed two-and-a-half hours away in Meerut, they thought it would be too risky to try to get them all in one operation.

Puja and Gita urged us to go as soon as we could to get the girls, saying, "The older Nanu and Kaya grow, the more at risk they are to being sexually exploited." They also saw an opportunity to use the fact that they were so very young to our advantage in the rescue. "When we were at the brothel, the *ma'am* did seem worried about being publicly exposed that she had underage children in the brothel. Even though she has a lot of control over the police and their raids, she knew that evidence of these young girls could cause her to be shut down by the government."

They shared with us that while the police were not always vigilant about monitoring the brothels, often were themselves *customers*, and frequently were part of the lucrative profits of the brothels, they were under pressure from the governmental and nongovernmental organizations to crack down on sex trafficking—particularly when underage girls were involved. Gita and Puja suggested we use that to our advantage in our attempts to bring the girls back to Kathmandu.

The rescue team of three set out. Once they reached New Delhi, they went directly to the Indian police to file a police report that there were underage girls being held at this brothel. My *aama* pressed the police to come with them and assist in the rescue of her young granddaughters. The police agreed to my mom's request, and later that day, they were on their way. They walked right in, demanding to speak to the *ma'am*.

When the *ma'am* saw the police, she appeared accommodating, but Bahadur said that her glare was fire-hot as she looked at Puja and my mom. He stayed as close to them as he could, knowing that the *ma'am* was going to pounce the moment she had the chance.

Puja did not want to give the *ma'am* time to hide or move the girls, so she pulled my mom out of the room where the police were talking with the *ma'am,* and they raced through the dark, crowded corridors. Bahadur, the strong man, stayed a few steps behind them for protection. They found the two girls, right where Puja had seen them last: Kaya, now five years old, was handing a beer to a man who was waiting his turn in the hallway, and Nanu, now four, was in a nearby room with other younger kids, surrounded by all kinds of foul garbage, including cigarette butts, beer bottles, and condoms. My mom swept up Kaya, Puja picked up Nanu, and they began to run.

The police were still in the brothel, but they had not yet caught up with our rescue team, who were fleeing with Nanu and Kaya. The race out of the brothel was a chaotic one. They fought hard to keep moving forward, whispering prayers for protection as they made their way. A few times, as they rounded corners or fled down dark hallways, they ran into brothel security guards. One security guard drew a gun and shot at my mom as she bolted away.

Aama sighed in wonder at the recollection and told me later, "Yes, they shot at me. But they missed, Hannah, and I kept running. Now that I finally had my granddaughters, I was a crazy person ... fighting, pushing, and running to get them to safety!"

My mom is still not sure exactly how they escaped and wondered if somehow the police had deterred the brothel security guards. When she and the others made it out to the streets below, they didn't slow down ... not one bit. They ran to the taxi they'd hired to wait for them, quickly piled in, and headed to the bus station.

Call it whatever you want, but I believe the only way to explain what happened is simple: this was a miracle.

Once in the relative safety of the bus, Mom told me that she held the girls close, singing to them and showing them pictures of the rest of their family, the school, and the dormitories that were waiting for them. She promised that she would return to India to get their mom as soon as she could. Understandably, initially, the girls were overwhelmed and confused, but they eventually nestled into the lap of their daring *hajuraama* (grandmother) and fell asleep.

Four days later, I returned to Kathmandu from Sweden. The minute our flight landed, I raced to find my nieces. We drove back to our dorm, and there they were. They were sitting together on the floor, watching a movie. I swept them into my arms, over the moon with excitement that they were safely here with us. Kissing their cheeks, I introduced myself, "I am Hannah, your auntie." They hugged me back shyly and then returned to their movie.

I sat down for a few minutes, filled with awe and gratitude that I was sitting in the same room with them. I began to dream of the moment that their mom—my *didi* Meena—would be here too. In my imagination, my sister and I sipped tea and talked quietly together, smiling at her boisterous children as they played and tumbled over one another.

Within a matter of days, my nieces latched on to Bina, their big sister. These three sisters formed a fast and tight bond and quickly became inseparable. Every time I saw them together, I smothered them with hugs and kisses, and they inevitably would fall to the floor in a volley of giggles. I couldn't help it. I was amazed and oh so thankful.

How these three loved their *aama*! They drew pictures of their mom, talked about her nonstop, and prayed together every day for her safe return to Kathmandu. Sometimes I sat with them and nodded along as they prayed, "Keep our *aama* safe and bring her home to us."

A Surprising Hello and Another Goodbye (2014)
3rd Rescue Team: Aama and Rajesh—Plan Crafted by Meena
In 2014, we found out from Chaha—Meena's pimp—that Meena had given birth to another baby. The day Chaha returned to our

village, she found my mom. "Auntie, I heard about your rescue last year of Meena's daughters and thought you'd want to know that Meena now has a son who is almost one year old. His name is Rahul."

Aama immediately called me and told me the news. At first, I doubted Chaha's story was true. I found her to be a fundamentally untrustworthy source. I thought she was up to her no-good-Chaha tricks. This was the one and the same Chaha who had deceived, abducted, and sold Puja, Gita, and Meena. But if this news was true—*satya*—we wanted to bring this baby boy back to us as soon as possible.

Chaha told my mom that she had left the brothel without permission, hoping to never return. "Life in the brothel is terrible. I hate it and don't want to go back. But I don't think I have a choice." She knew her family would not be happy that she had left without permission and was worried at what they would do to make sure she returned. "They are my family, yes. But they will be very angry. No one opposes them without punishment. If I am made to go back, I doubt I'll ever be able to leave again. This might be my only chance."

When one of the brothel's security guards arrived in the village the next day and found Chaha, she did not even put up a fight but quietly picked up her bag and followed him to the road leading away from our village.

A few days later, with a bit of caution and tentativeness, my mom traveled again—this time, alone—to New Delhi, determined to return with her infant grandson, Rahul. She had received a specific location of the home where Meena was staying and was anxious to see her daughter and meet her grandson.

Meena told me later about this moment. I want you to hear the story directly from my sister Meena of seeing our mom for the first time in nearly a dozen years.

Seeing Aama at Long Last (As Shared by Meena)
"Meena! There is a woman at the door for you!"

I wondered, *Who might this be?* Not many women came to our

brothel house in the poorest part of Meerut. Never did I imagine opening the door to see my *aama* standing there. I stood blinking in the sunlight. I was astounded.

My mom broke the silence. "Meena!" She was weeping. "My love, how I have missed you!"

I couldn't believe it. My *aama* was in India! I was fourteen when Chaha sold me to the brothel—twelve long years earlier—and I'd stopped hoping I'd ever see my mom again. Inviting her inside, we went upstairs and sat on my bed. I was happy to see that no one else was in the bedroom I shared with four other brothel workers, so we could talk in privacy.

She told me the story of her dogged determination to return to New Delhi over and over for me. "I was not giving up until I found you," she sighed as she took my hand in hers.

I had heard about her dramatic rescue of my daughters in the brothel on G.B. Road two years earlier. But as she told me more of the details, I was awestruck at the lengths my *aama* had gone for my children and me.

Looking around, she asked where Rahul was. "The *ma'am* took him back to G.B. Road. She didn't want us to grow too attached to each other or for me to become distracted from my work. I miss him so much. *Aama*, he hasn't even turned one yet. It breaks my heart. I have five beautiful children and yet not one of them lives with me." I began to weep, and my mom enwrapped me with her small—but mighty—arms.

When she asked if I wanted to see some pictures of our family, of course, I said, "*Ho!*" *Aama* pulled out her phone and showed me photos of Kaya and Nanu getting ready for school and playing with their friends. "And here is your Bina," my mom said, flipping to a picture of my eldest daughter. "She has been in Kathmandu with Hannah for the past five years, since she was nine years old. She's in school and is so smart, Meena. She has lots of friends, but do you know who she loves most right now? Her little sisters. They are inseparable." She showed me a picture of the three of them dancing together, their heads thrown back in laughter. "How they love and miss you. They dream to be with you again, my daughter."

Wow, I never thought they'd ever be together—in school now and looking so smart and nice, dreaming for me to be home with them? But, in a flash, humiliation eclipsed my happiness and sucked the momentary joy out of the room, leaving in its wake a profound sense of shame. The many ways I had failed my girls suddenly overwhelmed me, and I dropped my head self-consciously. I ached with grief.

As if my mom could read my mind, she said, "Meena, my love. Don't worry. Your girls are going to be okay. Your life has been full of more sorrow and sadness than anyone should ever have to endure. Dear one, you have done your best."

"*Aama,*" I whispered, "Who took care of Bina after I left for New Delhi so many years ago? Was it you?"

"*Ho,*" she nodded. "Yes, your dad and I took care of her until she went to Kathmandu to attend school. And we loved caring for her. She's a special girl. Your sisters Hannah and Aasha helped a lot too. You know how we are—we help each other. Caring for your daughter was no burden, my love."

I asked her to show me pictures of Hannah and Aasha. I was stunned and barely recognized my little sisters. Both were so beautiful. The way they dressed and held themselves with pride made them look more like *Bollywood* movie stars than the skinny and poor *Badi* girls I remembered.

My mom told me that Hannah was nearly finished with high school and was a leader, not just among our people but growing in her global influence to raise awareness about our people, about the realities of human trafficking, and about the change that is possible as an international community. She told me that Hannah would be leaving for a tour through the United States the following year. So much had transpired since we were last together!

When she told me that Aasha was in Kuwait for work and shared stories about the place in Kathmandu where Hannah and my girls were all living, I was struck by the ways in which each of us had followed promises for a fresh start; theirs were true and mine were not.

My mom knelt before me. "Meena, please come home. Your three girls are waiting for you there. What kind of life is this for your son? For you?"

I shook my head, "No, *Aama*, it is not possible. I cannot come home. This is my fate, and I cannot change it. I'm not ready to come, but would you take my chhora back to Nepal to be with his sisters and aunties? This is no place for a baby."

My mom didn't back down. "Of course, I will do what I can to bring your son home with me. But Meena, we love *you*. Hannah, your girls, and I will not rest until you are back in Kathmandu. Say yes and come with me now."

Tears filled my eyes. I allowed myself a moment to lean against my *aama*. As I did, I considered the hopelessness of the situation. I had repaid my debt and was free to leave, but there was nothing left for me. No hope. No dreams. Nothing in this lifetime. I didn't tell my mom the depths of my desperation, but simply said, "No, not now, *Aama*. I cannot do what you ask."

I also believed that it was safer for her to take Rahul back to Nepal without me. Just then, a clear strategy for how my mom could rescue my son came to mind. I spelled it out to my mom to the very last detail. "*Aama*, I know a man who will make the rescue possible. His name is Rajesh, and he's been coming to see me for ten years. Every time we meet, he tells me that he loves me and that he wants to marry me. I think he will do whatever I ask, and the *ma'am* will do whatever he asks. She is eager to please one of her most loyal *customers*."

After I spelled out every detail of the plan, my mom looked at me and nodded her acceptance. I hoped this would make for a successful and safe rescue of my Rahul.

Before she left, I talked honestly with her about one of my

deepest fears about going back to Nepal. "I cannot leave this place and return home because I have brought such great shame upon our family, upon you, *Aama*. I cannot bear to see the eyes of my sisters and of our village neighbors, hardened with judgment."

Aama held me close. "Meena, you are right. Yes, in our culture, honor is everything, and shame is pervasive. But our love for you is greater. You will feel no shame from your family. We've all been forced or chosen to do things that we regret." I closed my eyes and wanted to believe her. But in that moment, sadness enveloped me.

More than anything, I felt incapacitated by exhaustion.

I'd never told anyone, but I believed I was dying. I felt weaker by the day, and my bleeding never stopped. As if reading my thoughts, my mom said, "I'm worried about your health, my *chhori*. I don't know how much longer you will survive here. When you get to Kathmandu, you can get the medical care you need."

Hope flickered, and I whispered, "Okay, *Aama*, I'll think about it." I was again weeping. My mom held me and covered me with a prayer and a blessing, begging me to come with her. I shook my head. She sighed and asked me to confirm what I'd said, "Meena, at least promise you'll think about it?"

I nodded a tearful yes and walked my mom out of the house and into the blazing light of New Delhi's afternoon sun. In that moment, I didn't even notice the smell of the garbage-mountains surrounding us.

I hailed a rickshaw for my mom, and we said goodbye again. As she sped away, I could see in the back window that she had her phone to her ear. I was pretty sure she was calling Hannah, my brave *bahini*.

Picking up the phone, I called Rajesh, who answered on the first ring. He immediately said yes to my request to meet my mom at the brothel on G.B. Road and help her get Rahul back to Nepal.

After we hung up, I walked back into the house and collapsed in a heap. *What now? What next?* I wondered if I would ever see my sisters, mom, or children again.

I heard later from a friend of mine at the G.B. Road brothel about the very uneventful rescue of my son that day.

My mom and Rajesh walked into the brothel together. Rajesh told the *ma'am* that my mom was there to take Rahul back to Nepal. Playing a master-negotiator, Rajesh calmly told the *boss* that my mom had the backing of an influential NGO that was positioned to cause the brothel some very bad press if the *ma'am* didn't relinquish Rahul right away. He told her that if she handed over Rahul, the NGO said they wouldn't cause her any trouble.

The *ma'am* glared hard at my *aama* and smiled warmly at Rajesh. "Fine, take him. I'm glad to be done with Meena's children." Looking directly at my mom, she sneered, "He is an ugly *kukur* (dog), and we'll be better off without him."

With that, she called one of the girls to bring Rahul to my mom. Taking Rahul into her arms, my *aama* walked briskly out of the brothel with Rajesh at her side.

No guns. No shots fired. No fights. Just the cooing of her grandson, Rahul.

You're Not Taking Her! (2015)
1st Prevention Team: Hannah

Festivals in Nepal are, in many ways, the heartbeat of our community. I will always be grateful for the ways in which these celebrations opened a door for me to be my Hannah-warrior self to fight for Meena to return to us from the tractor brothers' house in India *and* for Gita and Puja to now live free in Kathmandu with me and our other sisters.

Sometimes, our festivals last for days, and other times, they go on for many weeks. Time itself seems to dance with the ebb and flow of our celebrations throughout the year. In our village, poor as we have been—perhaps even *because* of our poverty—we earnestly dive into each celebration … feasting, making music, and dancing with wild abandon. I cannot remember a time when it was not so.

Yet, I have repeatedly seen a dangerous and dark side to these festivals. Traffickers themselves know that girls often return home to be with their families. Not only are they crafty and opportunistic, but traffickers are intimately acquainted with our culture and community. Remember: they are often our next-door neighbor or very own family member. Thus, each festival becomes a lucrative—and relatively simple—business opportunity for those who are looking to traffic our girls. Over steaming cups of *chiya* and too many drinks of intoxicating *rakshi*, they stealthily lure parents into selling their girls or go straight to the girls themselves and offer lucrative work, promising a good life and high-paying jobs. The poorer our people have become, the more successful the traffickers. Hunger and desperation have made my people much less discerning and more vulnerable to lies and false promises.

In fact, I will tell you a tale of when this very thing happened, when a few friends of mine and I decided to leave Kathmandu and return to our village for the vibrant and colorful festival of *Holi*. While we can celebrate our festivals anywhere, we love to be home, most of all, for these special days.

As we walked down the hill and caught a glimpse of the tops of our village huts, we broke into a run, shouting breathless farewells to each other as we each peeled off, heading to our families' homes. Bursting into the door, I was ecstatic to see my *aama* and *buba*. After many hugs and greetings, Dad exclaimed, "Hannah *chhori*, you're twenty now … and, my love, how smart and beautiful you're looking!" Then, my mom asked me a flurry of questions. "How was the bus ride? How is school … your friends … your travel arrangements for the US tour? Are you still feeling healthy? No more headaches, dizziness?"

Although I'd been feeling no pain for six years now, they asked how I was feeling every time we were together or spoke on the phone. "Mom and Dad, I'm good. I'm happy. I feel *great*! Don't worry."

How good it was to be home! We spent our days busily preparing for the festival, cooking a few extra special dishes for the feast, making our simple home as clean as possible, and enjoying extended time together.

One morning, Jiya, one of my friends who had returned to the village with me from school in Kathmandu, burst into our home. She was giddy and glowing.

"Hannah sister, I have the best news ever! I'm getting married! Your cousin, Prayan, asked me to marry him ... and I said yes!"

Breathless and ecstatic, she continued telling me her story, talking a mile a minute, but I had stopped listening the moment she said *Prayan*. My mind was spinning and silently shouting *Nooooooo!* Prayan's mom, my Aunt Ditya, was a brothel owner. I didn't trust her—or Prayan. With every word Jiya spoke, I grew more and more angry, resolved, and protective. For years in Kathmandu, we'd been in school and living together in the dorms. She was just fifteen years old and had a bright future ahead of her.

This was another *recycled story* that I'd seen play out over and over. It went like this: A man tells a girl, "I love you. I'll take care of you. Marry me." After she says yes, things change. Every time. I've seen all kinds of variations with the same result that inevitably involves trickery, abuse, coercion, and ... well, rarely is it "happily ever after."

I knew she would end up at my aunt's brothel. Her sister had already gone missing, and rumor had it that she was at Prayan's family's brothel. No, I was sure of it—he didn't love her. He was using her, and she was under his spell. Like so many other girls, she had been brainwashed by love ... or by how she felt to be loved by a man. But this wasn't true love, I was sure of it. She would lose everything if she fell for his lies.

No doubt seeing my face looking more grim than enthusiastic, Jiya slowed down and finally stopped talking. Then she asked, "Hannah, what's wrong? You don't look happy. Why aren't you happy for me?"

I took a deep breath, trying to calm my thoughts and emotions. "Jiya, *bahini*, you're right. I am not happy. Not at all. Don't get me wrong. I want you to fall in love and get married if that's what you want. I want every single one of your wildest dreams to come true. But this is not the way. I know it. You are being lied to, and I don't trust him. You know Prayan's mom is the brothel *boss*, right? I think that the whole family is using you, and if you go with him, you will be in great danger."

Her rosy cheeks and big smile turned steely. Wordlessly, she turned on her heels and walked out of my house. I ran after her, begging her to reconsider. "Jiya, sister, please don't do this. He is no good for you." But she didn't believe me, lured in more by his attention and affection than the truth I spoke.

The next morning, I went to her house to try to talk with her some more. Her *aama* told me she wasn't there. "She left early this morning, and I'm not sure where she is."

"Oh, no!" I whispered. "No, no, no!" My heart began to race. The hair stood up on the back of my neck. I didn't know where she was, but I was determined to find her. I stormed through the village, shouting, "Jiya, where are you? Has anyone seen Prayan?"

I had heard that my Aunt Ditya, Prayan's mom, was back in the village for the festival. I marched up to her house and pounded on her door. As I battered on the door and demanded for her to open it, suddenly, as clear as day, I felt it. I knew it! *Jiya was inside Ditya's house.* I hit the door harder. Hollered louder. "Ditya Auntie, open the door! You're not taking Jiya. I see what you're doing. You've already taken her sister and now you think you can take Jiya. I'm not going to let you do this!"

I pressed my ear to the door and heard nothing. Taking a breath and saying a prayer, I resumed my impassioned pounding. "I'm not going away. You are not getting away with this. Not this time. Let me in. Now!"

The villagers had started gathering to see what would happen next. No one had ever stood up to Ditya before. She was rich. She was powerful. And she was dangerous.

Finally, I heard footsteps. Ditya opened the door and stood

before me with an air both condescending and confident. "Hannah, what's the trouble? Why the pounding and the shouting?" Her words were silky and smooth, but her eyes were undeniably evil. "I'm sorry, Hannah, Jiya isn't here. You're too late. She left with your cousin hours ago. She's long gone."

With that, she stepped onto the front porch, shutting the door behind her. I thought, *Oh, no. I don't think so. That closed door is not going to stop me from getting to Jiya.* I took a step toward Ditya, raising my chin in wordless defiance. I stood just inches from her face and looked her straight in the eye. I forcibly shoved her aside. As I moved past her, she grabbed my arm. Still not free of her grasp, but undeterred, I raised my leg and kicked the door with all my strength. Hardware from the metal door clattered to the floor, and the door stood slightly ajar.

In a flash, I lunged into the house, yelling, "Jiya! I know you're here. Where are you?" I ran through the house quickly, crying Jiya's name as I went. Ditya stayed by the front door, cursing and taunting me. It was the biggest house in our village, but it still didn't take long to make my way through it. The final place to look was the kitchen. I thought to myself, *I hope Jiya is here. What am I going to do if she's not?*

As I walked around the kitchen, I nearly tripped over her as she crouched and trembled behind a wall. I didn't know if she was hiding from me or wanting to be found by me, but it didn't matter. She was not going anywhere.

I pulled her up and out to the front door, holding her shirt. I stood toe to toe with Ditya but spoke to Jiya, loudly enough for the whole village to hear what I was saying. "You are not allowed to get married. You're only fifteen years old, Jiya. My cousin and aunt will ruin you and destroy your future, just like they have your sister's. You are one of the lucky ones right now, in school and with a good future ahead."

Ditya looked unworried, standing before me like a bodyguard, imposing and daring me to try to get past her. Lunging fast, she slapped me a few times at first, and then the blows came harder and faster. One-handed, I defended myself and fought back, still holding onto Jiya with my other hand. I was determined to get Jiya to safety, away from this house. Ditya was strong, but in that moment, I was stronger. As I forced my way past her, she screamed and, in a rage, ripped my shirt in two. "Devisara—or now, am I to call you *Hannah*?—you're going to regret this. You'd better watch your back."

Pulling Jiya with me, I ran with all my might to my house. I didn't care that the neighbors were laughing and leering. Once we reached my house, I discovered why the neighbors mocked me. My shirt was in tatters, my hair was in disarray, and I had red marks all over my face from her slaps and punches. Right then, it didn't matter. I exhaled, looked at Jiya with a warning expression to stay right where she was, and started making some tea.

That night, I slept with my arm linked to Jiya's. I was resolute. She was not going anywhere. The next morning, we left by bus and returned to Kathmandu, out of the reach of my aunt and cousin.

On the long bus ride, I went over in my mind what had just happened. If I hadn't been there, Jiya would now be headed to G.B. Road. I shuddered at the thought. Disturbed and angered by the many ways I have seen girls so easily manipulated by men, it struck me that all it seemed to take was for a man to paint a picture of love—like a fairy tale. The words *love* and *marriage* seemed to make a girl lose all intellectual capacity and become blind to seeing whether a man was promising something he could truly provide.

But part of me understood. In my village, women are hungry. Hungry for food. Hungry for love. This dual hunger seems to make them twice as vulnerable. Men seemed to play with and be able to control women's hunger and vulnerability. And women seem to lose every time.

Logically, I considered that not every man was opportunistic and manipulative. I hoped there were exceptions to my sweeping gener-alizations, but I'd not yet seen any. *Someday,* I thought, *maybe I will find love. But for now, I will fly high and do what I can to stay safely above this losing love game.*

Jiya and I made it safely back to Kathmandu. She came to me every day for weeks, sometimes wordlessly sharing her gratitude with a smile or a hug and other times crying as her words of thanks tumbled over each other. She realized she had been saved from a horrifying life in the brothels of India and was lucky to, instead, be back in school with a future that glittered brightly.

Beaten Up and Left to Die (2015)
2nd Prevention Team: Mystery Man

On a rainy afternoon near dusk, I walked home from school alone. I heard the rumble of motorcycles approach and then stop some distance behind me. A moment later, the engines thundered back to life. Looking over my shoulder, I saw two motorcycles racing toward me.

This was not a good situation—I was all by myself, and the night was fast approaching; it was nearly dark. My heart racing, I started to walk faster. As the motorcycles overtook me, they positioned themselves on either side of me—one on my right and the other on my left. One man, who was sitting on the back of one of the bikes, forcibly grabbed my backpack and held me suspended above the ground.

I yelled, "Why are you doing this? Who are you?" Hoping I didn't sound as terrified as I was, I tried to make my voice rise above the roar of the motorcycles and hoped that someone nearby would hear me.

One man quickly shot back, "You and your *Badi* people need to get out of here, leave our neighborhood and leave *soon*. You are nothing—worthless. A mangy dog is more valuable. Go back to your village, *Badi* girl."

They got off their bikes, pushed me to the ground, and began to beat me. I covered my head and curled up in a ball, doing what I could to protect myself from their violent kicks and blows.

In the tumult, the motorcycle men began to argue about whether to leave me on the street or take me with them. But just then, I heard a voice, "She's just a girl. Let the *keti* go." One of the men shouted back, "No!"

Their blows slowed, and in a moment, they stopped entirely. I couldn't believe it, but this stranger's command seemed to have interrupted them in such a way that their plans to cause me harm were hindered ... at least, that day, they were.

A moment later, I heard them get on their bikes. But before they sped off, one of the motorcycle men leaned down and growled with disdain and fierce anger into my ear, "I'm going to kill you someday. You cannot run and hide forever. Next time, you won't have this man to save you. I'll come back. I'll find you, Devisara Hannah *Badi*."

A cloud of dust enveloped me as they sped away, and for a moment, I stayed curled up in a tight ball on the ground. But I knew I had to rally. *What if they come back? You've got to get out of here, Hannah!* I willed myself to move. Pulling myself upright, I first began to walk, and I then picked up my pace. With what seemed to be supernatural energy, I ran for my life. When I arrived at my dormitory, I beat on the door and shouted for someone to let me in. As the caretaker opened the door, I took a step inside and then fell to the ground, unconscious.

The next morning, I woke up with the faces of my sisters surrounding me. They were worried and curious. "Hannah, *didi*, what happened?" "Who did this to you?" As I told them my story, I thought about the man who prevented the motorcycle men from accomplishing their bad plans for me. It's true, he saved me. And yet, I wondered, *Why didn't he do more? Was it because he heard I was* Badi?

Why did he leave me, injured and alone, on the sidewalk? Whatever the reason, it didn't seem right. It doesn't seem like a good way to treat another human being, regardless of their caste or last name.

Meena Escapes the Brothel (2015)
4th Rescue Team: Aama Maya and Rajesh

It was time to leave Nepal for an international tour to talk about human trafficking and promote a film about our people. Before leaving for the airport, I kissed my nieces goodbye and told them I'd bring back some special treats for them.

Was I excited? Oh, my goodness, *ho!* Yes, this was the trip of a lifetime, and I was over the moon as we boarded the plane. Curiosity was in my blood! I imagined the places we'd visit and the people we'd meet. I was born for adventure, to fight for justice, and to speak with people about what matters most to me, so the days ahead seemed like a spectacular combination of my very favorite things.

Minutes before the wheels touched down in New Delhi, where we had a brief layover before heading to the United States, the plane's window gave me a spectacular view of the third largest city in the world. My eyes panned over the tall buildings surrounded by a massive cluster of aluminum-roofed shacks, tents in tatters, and mountains of garbage. As I took in Delhi's many complicated traffic arteries, I imagined them jam-packed with rickshaws and trucks, a throng of pedestrians pressed together in a mighty mass of movement.

While I was in awe at the size and sprawl of this city of twenty-five million people, in that moment, I only thought of one. My sister Meena was down there, somewhere, amid the many millions. I clenched my hands into fists, closed my eyes, and begged God to give me strength for the fight ahead. I dreamed of the day I'd be in the city below, with my sister safely in my charge. I felt a deep sense of peace pervade my mind and my heart. *Trust, Hannah. Your sister will be all right. Do not worry.* I took a deep breath and turned my attention to the days ahead.

There was little time to think of anything else, for the moment we arrived in the United States, our days were full to the brim! In six weeks, we hopped on planes that took us to California, Texas, and Colorado. We spoke at universities, churches, and homes; saw mountains and the ocean; rode bikes for the first time; and met extraordinary people. *Ho,* I felt happy and free … I was having an adventure of a lifetime!

As we headed to Minnesota, with just a few more stops left during our US tour, my *aama* called. She was so excited that she wasn't speaking clearly; I had a hard time understanding her. She had to repeat herself a few times, but I finally understood. "Meena said yes! I'm going to New Delhi to bring your sister home. I am going as soon as I can. I don't want to wait a moment longer."

Holding the phone in my hand, I sat there in stunned and grateful silence. *Meena is coming home. She might even be in Nepal by the time we get back from the United States.*

I remembered the gathering we'd had together with Sarah and some of her family and friends in Denver—her community that quickly felt like family. I had tearfully told them about Meena, and we prayed together that she would decide to come home, to have a change of heart. This was exactly what we had hoped, dreamed, and prayed for!

My mom promised to keep me informed of her progress and whereabouts. Once again, she told me that Meena had suggested we ask Rajesh to assist, since he had been so helpful with Rahul's rescue. She believed he was trustworthy and committed to doing anything she asked. "Meena said that the *ma'am* allows him to take her wherever he likes around the city, making him the perfect 'cover' to get her out of New Delhi. Meena is confident that the *ma'am* will do whatever she can to keep him a happy and frequent *customer.*"

My mom told me later that by the time she made it to Delhi,

Meena and Rajesh were ready and had solidified their plan. They agreed that it was best for *Aama* to remain unseen, since she was now known by the brothel strong man and *ma'am*. They didn't want to cause the brothel security to be wary and, therefore, more watchful of Meena.

Rajesh was eager to help Meena escape if she agreed that he could go to Nepal with her. He told her that his dream was to start a new life with her in Kathmandu and begged her to consider again his marriage proposal. Meena said she would think about it once they made it safely back to Nepal.

Once again, Meena will tell her story here, in her own words.

Finally Free from Delhi (As Shared by Meena)

The day dawned bright and warm—the sky hazy with New Delhi's thick pollution. As I showered and got dressed, I wondered, *Could this be my last morning in this brothel?* Rajesh had called the *ma'am* to tell her that he wanted to take me to a hotel that night and would send a rickshaw for me at 7:00 p.m. "I'll have her back in the morning, at the usual time," he promised. She'd called me to tell me to be ready that night for my most regular *customer*.

I pretended to prepare myself as I always did and got dressed in my best *sari* and put on my makeup. As I looked at myself in the mirror, I saw it in my own eyes: a glimmer of hope, of possibility. Tightening my jaw, I shook my head and willed myself not to be preoccupied or distracted with the dream of being in Nepal with my children. *Focus first on your escape. If you cannot get out of here this time, you will never see them. This is it, your only chance.*

Shortly after 7:00 p.m., as promised, I heard the putt-putt of the rickshaw approaching and gathered my things to head out for the night. I got in, sat down, and I was off. I was headed to G.B. Road, toward the hotel that Rajesh always booked for us. The drive was long. It took nearly two hours to get there from Meerut. As the rickshaw drove into G.B. Road's muggy and thronging night, flashbacks—mostly awful and repulsive—from the last thirteen years washed over me. I brushed tears away from my cheeks and kept my eyes on the road ahead, willing myself to keep any emotions at bay. *Focus, Meena. Focus.*

Finally, I made it to the place I was to meet Rajesh and my *aama*. It was a quiet and, we hoped, safely hidden alley of shops near the hotel.

I exhaled with relief to see that they were right where we'd planned to meet, and as Rajesh helped me into the cab, I slid into my mom's embrace. Wordlessly, she wrapped her arms around me and held me close as we sped away from G.B. Road toward the bus station.

We boarded the bus without incident, and after we made it past the border between India and Nepal, I began to breathe a bit easier as our bus lumbered—one mile at a time—closer to Kathmandu and my children.

There was a moment I'll never forget during the bus ride, when I awoke to find my mom sleeping next to me. As I gazed in quiet wonder at her, I thought, *How strong you are, Aama.* This was her third rescue. Three times, she risked her life for ours. *First my girls, then my boy, and now me.* As I looked at her, it dawned on me: *She is my hero.*

After three days on the bus, we pulled into Nepal's capital city, and Hannah's friends took me straight to the hospital. Back from her US tour, my ever-the-fighting little sister Hannah came directly from the airport to visit me in the hospital. Weeping, she hugged me and said, "Welcome home, Meena *didi*." She didn't leave my side, a standing sentinel to protect her big sister.

Two days later, I was discharged with strict requirements to rest and return for regular checkups. I knew I was lucky. I had tested negative for HIV and would continue to be treated for my bleeding.

Straightaway, Hannah took me to meet my children. As we drove toward them, she explained, "Meena sister, there are now hundreds of *Dalit*—and many *Badi*—children being housed and educated in Kathmandu. It's awesome! And more kids want to come, so we're growing as fast as we can." With quiet joy and wise insight, she then said, "We also thought that it might be nice for you to have a few days just to be with your kids, without the crazy noise and energy of the dormitories. You can stay with your children in the home of one of my friends for a few weeks. When you are ready, I'll take you to see where your kids have been living and going to school."

I was amazed and grateful for some time to be alone with my kids. It had been one year since I'd seen Rahul, three since I'd seen Nanu and Kaya, and thirteen since I'd seen Bina.

As Hannah and I walked in, Nanu and Kaya ran up to me, burying their faces in my *sari* skirt. Bina stood by quietly, and Rahul cocked his head quizzically as he looked up at me. When I sat down, Kaya and Nanu piled into my lap, and Bina came to sit with us. I looked at her, stroked her cheeks and hair, and said, "Bina my love, my *chhori*, it is so good to see you. My daughter, you have grown so big and so beautiful." As I spoke to her, I saw her eyes soften and tear up. She scooted closer and put her head on my chest.

We had dinner together that first night. Afterward, I took a shower, using a mango-smelling shampoo Hannah had purchased for me, before piling into bed with my kids. "*Aama*," Kaya said, "I love the smell of your hair!" Then they nestled in as close as they could, and one by one, each of my four children fell asleep, their sweet breath and smells flooding my senses. I was exhausted ... but too much in awe at the miracle of this moment to sleep just yet. I willed myself to stay awake so I could keep looking at their sweet faces and stroke their hair with wonder. This was the first night we'd all been together at bedtime. It was the first night in my life when I remembered falling asleep in peace.

Once I did fall asleep, I was awakened once, then twice, then again and again, by one of my kids kissing my cheeks or rubbing my arm or nestling closer—sometimes in their sleep and sometimes in that in-between place of wakefulness.

Almost Trafficked, Again (2016)
3rd Prevention Team: Dormitory Staff

As I recovered from jet lag and the whirl of my US tour, the days after Meena returned to Kathmandu were busy for her, with medical checkups, diligently taking medicine for her illness, receiving trauma counseling and therapy, learning how to speak Nepali again (she'd spoken Hindi for most of her life), and—her favorite—spending time with her children. But one month later, there was a terrifying and nearly catastrophic occurrence: Meena was almost trafficked, again.

Rajesh, the man who avowed his love for Meena, helping to rescue both her son *and* her, had stayed in Kathmandu. Watching him closely, I thought he seemed to be a pretty good guy who loved my sister. We were impressed by his dedication to Meena. When asked how she felt about him, Meena was shy but said she was happy.

Meena told me that he often tried to convince her to return to India with him. He wanted to go back but didn't want to leave without Meena. He promised her that if she went back, it wouldn't be to work in the brothel, but to be married and live a good life, together. Over and over, he begged and pleaded for her to say yes. Over and over, she told him no. "I do not want to be separated from my kids again, after all of these years. No, I will not go back."

One day, he came to her room in the dormitory, begging and pleading once more. Again, she said no. This time, his eyes grew angry, and he lunged at her, holding her down to the ground as he snarled his demands and threatened the safety of her children. Terrified, Meena whispered no, again. He went crazy and said, "Meena, you have no choice. I'm taking you whether you want to come or not." He punched her over and over, striking her stomach and her face with great force. Before she blacked out, she yelled for help. He tried to muffle her shouts. As she passed out, one of the caretakers of the dormitory burst into the room.

Rajesh fled. Meena was bleeding badly from a gash over her eye and had major pain from the blows to her stomach, so she was taken to the hospital. She needed stitches and pain medicine, but that night, she again slept with her arms around her children, piled one over the other in a cozy bundle of momma love.

Rajesh hasn't been seen since, and Meena hasn't heard from him.

As Meena slowly recovered, I asked her, "Why do you think that Rajesh changed from being your rescuer to your abuser? Why would he suddenly morph from one who loved you and risked so much to save you and Rahul to one who violently beat you unconscious?"

Meena was quiet but slowly began to speak. "Hannah *bahini*, although I think he may have loved me, do not forget that he has paid to have sex with me for ten years. He has a lot of money and power. I don't think he's used to being told 'No,' certainly not from a low-caste *Badi* woman like me. I think he went crazy because he couldn't buy and have what he wanted."

We grew quiet, sitting with Meena's words. I scooted closer to her. "*Didi*, I'm so thankful that you and your children are no longer powerless, no longer at risk to be bought and owned by men. You are strong and so very, very brave. I love you."

The 21 Children (2016)
5th Rescue Team: Raju, Meena, Hannah, Two Badis, and Two Pimps

Just a few months after Meena's rescue, she told me she wanted to go back to New Delhi. Some children were there in a home in a very poor area near the Ghazipur garbage dump. "Hannah *bahini*, these are some of Delhi's largest, most dangerous, and most impoverished places, located just fifteen minutes from G.B. Road. In it lies a brothel where many of the young children of the sex workers are kept. I remember the moment I saw these kids—mostly small girls—for the first time, and I cannot get them out of my head. You thought that G.B. Road and Meerut were bad? This place is even worse, if you can believe it."

She went on to tell me about the nearly thirty-acre garbage heap that many call "Trash Mountain." "It releases toxins into the air and contaminates the water." She spoke about the many children she saw digging in the trash, looking for anything of value they could sell for food.

"Hannah, men come every day to have sex with the mothers, but sometimes they choose these children instead. They are so little. It makes me sick to think about it. I want to get them and bring them back to us, here in Kathmandu. What do you think? Can we do it, and will you help?"

I looked at Meena and nodded wordlessly. *What else is there to say in response to such a request ... to this news?* I sat there in awe of her strength. "Meena, there is no one in the whole world more resilient and braver than you, *didi.*"

I said yes. Right away, we went into planning mode and put together our team, including two trusted *Badi* sisters, Raju Uncle, Meena, and me. Meena planned to ask two women pimps to help too. We would investigate that possibility once we got to India. Meena said that if we were successful, we would return with twenty children.

We traveled to Anand Vihar, a district in the outskirts of New Delhi, in the spring of 2016. Our plan required that we first spend time building trust with the children, with their mothers, and with the brothel *ma'am.*

First, we knew we needed someone on the "inside" of the brothel where the kids were staying. Meena approached two women pimps who oversaw handling the *customers* who wanted to hire young girls for sex. Meena was smart—she knew they worried that if they were found out by the police, they would be arrested and sent to jail for keeping underage *workers*. They agreed to help us if we promised not to report them to the police.

Next, the brothel *ma'am*. The day after we arrived, a team member and I approached her and said we were with a child advocacy NGO. "We are here to ensure that the living conditions for the children of the brothel workers are acceptable—and have some grant money to make improvements, if needed." Money always seemed to be a reliable motivator, and she granted us permission to "assess" the condition of the house.

Returning to the *ma'am* the next day with a report of what we found at the brothel, we issued a grave warning and an easy solution. "This is no good for you or your business. The twenty-one children of the women in your Anand Vihar brothel are dirty, have few clothes, and aren't eating well. We'd like to take them to buy some clothes and shoes and buy them food. It will cost you nothing. We will provide everything. If you say no, we will report you to the government." We counted on the fact that even here, in the brothel, there was a desire for honor and respect ... and to keep her lucrative brothel open without interruption.

She said yes and gave us permission to take them out each day for one week. Every morning, we arrived at the brothel and began the challenging task of corralling all twenty-one children into rickshaws, taking them in and out of markets. We purchased twenty-one pairs of shoes and twenty-one new outfits. They savored food and tasty sweets they had never eaten.

As we shopped and ate, we painted a picture of a future of freedom—which we believed and hoped would someday be theirs. We told the children that Meena's daughters and son had already made their way out of Delhi and now lived in Kathmandu together with us, after being born on G.B. Road. We showed them pictures of the girls at school doing their schoolwork and playing with their friends. We tried to build a sense of what was possible for them to experience beyond their limited lives in the brothel. But we didn't tell them that they could come with us until the morning of our departure.

Each night, we returned them safely to the brothel shack as promised, and sometimes we had dinner with them. The children's mothers often came to see their kids before their work at night and returned in the early hours of the morning whenever they could. We wanted to be able to share with the mothers how life was for the children who lived in Kathmandu, planting seeds for the moment we would offer to bring their kids with us to Kathmandu.

The more we were with them in the brothel, the more we understood how important it was for us to succeed in our mission. The shack where the children stayed was in shambles. It shook with every step, and we worried it would collapse at any moment. It was in a precarious place, surrounded by garbage, an open sewer, dangerous and desperate characters, and constant violence.

Men came and went all day and night. These children were abused, some forced to have sex when they were as young as four years old. We were resolute—we would not leave without them.

When we were not with the kids, we were busy doing whatever we could to ensure the success of the rescue. There was much to do. We went to the embassies of India and Nepal and got the necessary paperwork prepared for our travel back to Nepal. We booked a bus for the three-day trip. We talked with anti-trafficking organizations and created a larger network of support. We spoke to the police, making sure they knew that the embassies and NGOs had been notified of our plan, hoping this would keep any officers connected with the *ma'am* from telling her about the operation. We tried to stay one strategic power-move ahead of anyone who might stand in our way.

The day of the rescue, our team arrived at the brothel bright and early, at the same time as in days' past. The day before, we had told the mothers of the children—most of whom seemed far too young to be mothers—that we had special gifts for them and something important we wanted to talk with them about. We asked if they could meet us the following morning.

Once we were all together, I took a deep breath, said a prayer, and then asked, "We would like to bring your children with us to Kathmandu. Would you be willing to part with them so they can be safe, go to school, eat good meals, and be well cared for by our community? For those of you who wish to leave, we promise to come back for you as soon as we can."

We told them that they could take a little bit of time to think about it and talk with each other and their children before making their decision. Meena reminded them that we couldn't wait long. "There isn't much time. We have to leave in just one hour." We didn't want anyone—not even one of these mothers—to sound the alarm and alert the powers that be in the brothel of our plans.

One by one, each *aama* said yes. As we had gotten to know the kids, we found out that two of the youngest girls were daughters of the two pimps who were helping us on the inside. They, too, said *ho.*

The mothers helped their children pack the few belongings they owned, gave them kisses, and said their farewells. Tears flowed as the children piled again into the rickshaws. It looked as if we were bound for some city adventure as we had done for the past week. The rickshaws' motors whirred and buzzed us through the congested streets. Seeing that no one was following us, we made our way to the spot where the bus was parked.

We pulled around the corner and saw the large bus, ready and waiting. One by one, the children exited the rickshaws and stepped into the bus. It was a private, air-conditioned bus, quite unlike anything they had seen before. They ran up and down the aisles and looked out the windows at the busy streets around us as the bus lumbered along and made its way out of New Delhi.

The three-day bus ride from India to Nepal was anything but easy. Many of the children became motion sick, crying at their aching tummies and vomiting out the windows. Other children wailed with anxiety and worry.

"Where is my *aama?*"

"I want to go back!"

"Where are we going?"

These kids were traumatized. Most had been used and abused by men and had seen things most children would—thankfully—never see. Now they were traveling far away from their moms and familiar surroundings, in a bus bound for an unknown city, companioned by strangers. It was no wonder they were scared.

Finally, we made it safely to Kathmandu. As they piled off the bus, many of the children had tear-streaked cheeks and puffy eyes. They were free from the terrors of the brothels of G.B. Road, but their transition would require a lot of tender loving care and professional support from our trauma counselors and caretakers.

Immediately, Meena's children offered the sort of "therapy" only children can share with each other, as they ran out of the dormitory, first giving big hugs to their *aama*, and then, with curiosity and warmth, inviting the new children to come in and play.

Khushi: The Dancing Dreamer

A Fateful Errand (2016)

People tell me I am kind and that my eyes smile when I talk. My big dreams are to be a famous *Bollywood* dancer, to finish high school, and to help those who are hungry and homeless. I have known both—hunger and homelessness—all too well.

I am the only storyteller in this book who is not *Badi*. I am *Paraiyar*, also considered a *Dalit*—an *untouchable*. As my sisters have shared, within the *untouchables*, there is a hierarchy. *Badi* is at the bottom. *Paraiyar*, while *Dalit*, is a little higher in social standing, but not by much.

For years, my family and I lived in a very poor district called Bardiya. Each time my *aama* gave birth to a daughter, my *buba* threatened to leave her. Life was hard and grew even more difficult when my mom became terribly sick with epilepsy. We had no money for doctors or medicine. Her sickness burdened my dad, and when I—her sixth daughter—was born, my dad left the house in a rage, saying, "I will find a woman who is healthy and who can bear me a son." He never returned.

Life became harder than ever for us. I watched my sick mom struggle to care for all of us by herself. No matter how hard she worked, we never had enough. We were hungry all the time. Even though my dad left us, my heart ached for my *buba* to return, for a sense of wholeness in our family, and for the feeling of security his presence brought me. In Bardiya, violence was an everyday occurrence. I felt defenseless and vulnerable in our household of poor women and girls who had nothing.

When I was ten years old, my mom decided that the only way we could survive was to move back into her mother's house with my five sisters and me. The living quarters were tight, as my grandmother's small home already housed eight other people.

For years, life continued to be very, very hard. Every day was full of worry from sunup to sundown. Mostly, I worried that my mom would die. When she couldn't get out of bed because she was in too much pain or too weak, I would step outside and cry. I did not want her to be burdened by my tears. Although I had no idea how I could come up with the money she needed for her medicine and doctor visits, I was filled with an almost obsessive determination to find a way to help her. How I wanted her to feel better!

When I was thirteen, I went on an errand that would change my life. *Aama* had asked me to go to the market to buy some rice for dinner. As I shopped, a woman approached me and began to talk to me. "*Namaste, keti.* Little girl, you have very good luck today! I know of a cheaper shopping place not far from here. You will get much better prices there. I'm going there anyway, and you're welcome to come with me. We won't be gone long." She seemed friendly, and I was filled with excitement at the prospect that if I saved some money at the market, I could buy medicine for my mom.

As we went toward the cheaper market, we passed a *chiya* stand. She offered to buy me a cup of tea and some food. As usual, I was hungry, so I said yes. The food tasted delicious, and the tea was a rare treat ... but in a few minutes, the world went foggy and then black.

Death Would Be Better than This

When I woke up, disoriented and confused, I found myself in an unfamiliar place, in a room full of girls. *Where am I? Who are these other girls? Why am I here?* Someone told me that the woman in the market had drugged me, then sold me to a trafficker who would take me to a brothel in India. I didn't know it yet, but I was bound for the very same brothel where Meena, Gita, Puja, Aasha, and Sakhira had been enslaved. When I first arrived at the brothel on G.B. Road, I didn't know who they were or the miracle of their rescues. In the beginning, I was alone, without a trusted person in sight or hope of a way out.

Sex was everywhere. I did not understand this life—or what was expected of me. For a time, I just watched and tried to make sense of what surrounded me. I observed the girls in the brothel as they got ready for their *customers*, as they put on makeup and skimpy outfits. Then, the men came. At all times of the day and night. It was a whole new world, and I did not want it.

I was kept in a locked concrete room with other small girls. During my first few days at the brothel, I called for help over and over, shouting day and night for someone to come. I doubted it would do anything or that anyone could or would save me. But I had to try. I had to do something to get home to my mom and sisters.

One day, a scary, strong man came into my cell after hearing my persistent shouts. He grabbed my face and pressed his lips to my ear, snarling, "If you don't shush up and do your job, pretty little Khushi, I'll cut your body in pieces. I've done it before, and I'll do it again. No one will know or care that you're dead."

He then dragged me to face the *ma'am*. As I entered the room, she turned to look at me, her eyes gleaming with disdain and darkness. "I hear you're causing trouble, little one. You need to learn to shut up and do what you're told. Maybe this will teach you."

As she spoke, she picked up a spoon and held it over the blue-blazing fire of a gas burner. As she stepped toward me, the spoon glowing with heat, and I realized what she was about to do. The strong man tightened his grip on my shoulders, holding me still, as she pressed the spoon into the tender flesh of my arms and my shoulder. Her eyes narrowed with nasty pleasure as I screamed, agony flooding my body.

It didn't take long for me to stop shouting and yelling. I believed the only way I would survive was to do what they told me to do.

I began *working* the next day.

I had no choice. I was forced to sleep with twenty or thirty men a night ... sometimes more and sometimes less. It was painful beyond description. I could never get any rest. It was a revolving door of men. The men were different ages—some were as young as teenagers and others were as old as grandfathers—but they all wanted the same thing: to have sex with me ... a small and innocent-looking thirteen-year-old girl. I lived trapped and enslaved in a tiny, padlocked cement cell when I wasn't *working*, surrounded by other girls with the same bad luck and fate.

I tried to escape a few times but was caught by the strong man each time. He seemed to be everywhere, always one step ahead of me or able to catch me without even breaking a sweat. Each time, he dragged me directly to the *ma'am*, where the fiery hot coal-spoon and *ma'am's* fury awaited me.

"Khushi, you're such a fool," she'd spew at me. "Why do you even try to run away? You think someday you'll marry? Hah—no! If you get married, we *will* find you. We will tell your husband what is true: that you are a whore and have slept with thirty, forty, even fifty men a night. We will tell him that you were addicted to alcohol, drugs, *and* sex. And we won't stop with him—we will also tell your family ... everyone who knows you. They won't want you. No one will. All will hate you. Judge you. Oh, the shame of it all. At least here, we want you. At least here, you have a place to live. There is no life for you outside this brothel. Stop running—what is it for, anyway?"

Bistarai, bistarai, I began to agree with her. Slowly, slowly, I decided that the only way to stay alive would be to submit to the *ma'am* and stop trying to escape.

Men often gave me extra money. But it was never mine to keep. After every few *customers*, the *ma'am* would come to me and hold out her hand. "Khushi, give me your money. All of it. This is not your money to keep. Never forget it. I am the *boss*; you and your money belong to me."

I tried a few times to hide money from her in the folds of my *sari* skirt or wad it up in my hair and secure it with a clip, but she found it every time. She made me take off every item of clothing and stand naked in front of her. Running her hands through my hair, shaking out my clothing, looking into any places on my body where she thought I may have hidden money, she searched me thoroughly. She knew well the tricks we *foolish girls* might try. She'd had a lifetime of practice and had been trained well. Before her, it was her own *aama* who had been the *ma'am* of this brothel.

If she decided I had earned enough money and she was pleased with me, she gave me a few *rupees* to buy some rice. Hunger seemed to be my fate, as my stomach rumbled day and night. I often felt weak and dizzy from the many *customers* and not enough food.

I began to have a bleeding problem from being used and abused by far too many men. It wouldn't stop … nor would they. I started to think that maybe I would die from this bleeding. *That would be a relief*, I thought. I began to wish for death. Surely death would be better than this.

Dare I Trust Them? (2017)

I was little for my age, a particularly small thirteen-year-old. I learned quickly that many men liked little girls, which made me a lucrative commodity. But it also made me a risky one for the *ma'am*. When the brothel raids happened, the police were often tasked—and incentivized—to find underage girls. And if young girls were discovered, the brothel received a hefty fine.

One night, a new man entered the brothel. Scanning his options for the night, he pointed at and chose me, paying extra for a private room. When the door closed, he asked me what my name was. *How odd*, I thought. *I can't remember the last time someone asked my name.* Then he told me, "I don't want to have sex, Khushi. I just want to talk." *What? Why would he come, if not to have sex?* I was suspicious and doubtful.

But he came back the next night, and many nights after. Each time, he did the same thing. He never touched me—not once—and, paying extra for a private room, once we were alone, he would sit on one side of the room across from me and ask me many questions. "How did you get here? Where did you come from? How old are you? How do they treat you?"

I had never been able to tell anyone in the brothel my story before. Not only did no one seem to care, but we were simply not allowed to talk to one another, to share our stories. But *bistarai*, I told him mine. Slowly, I found the courage to ask him why he was there, paying money just to hear a story.

"Khushi, I am here because I love God. And God has put a passion in my heart to do what I can for you and the other girls who are stuck in this terrible place." I'd heard stories about many gods, but this one sounded different. He told many stories about his God, and although I didn't understand it, I felt flickers of hope in my heart. I thought, *Maybe someday, God might help me.*

One night, he told me that he'd like to take me away from this place, saying, "If you want to be free, Khushi, I will do everything I can to help you escape. This is not going to be the end of your story. I promise." Although initially, I was filled with excitement at the prospect of having help to leave this place, as I thought about it, I became more suspicious. I was in a quandary, and I wondered, *Can I trust him? Is he able to help me leave this place?* Although he'd given me no reason to doubt him and he had thus far treated me well, I had been promised many things by many people and lied to more times than I could count.

One day, shortly after he made his promise, I heard some of the girls saying that the police were planning a raid. Apparently, they had received a tip that there were some underage girls at the brothel. I wondered if the man who always talked about God had anything to do with it.

I would never know the answer to that question, nor would I ever see the *God-man* again, because the brothel *boss* had also heard about the raid. She decided to move me and a few other young and small girls to a different place. That night, a big man with a turban on his head came to take us to the new brothel. His name was Munna. His eyes looked evil, and I was scared. Although his religion didn't permit him to touch me, he issued his demands with a commanding voice that made me shudder: "Sit here. Don't talk—not one word. You'll regret it."

Like the *ma'am*, he had power that frightened me. I trembled and tried to do everything he asked. If I did not, I knew I would be in big trouble. I'd become good at doing as I was told. My life had depended on it.

We arrived at a new brothel. My hopes of it being a better place were quickly snuffed out. I immediately learned that the same family ran this place, and it was just as awful as the last one.

Four months passed. I grew more depressed and hopeless than ever. But one day, as I was doing laundry on the roof, I was shocked to hear my language being spoken. Curious, I made my way through the long fabric pieces of hanging *saris* and found a man and a woman standing together on the roof, quietly speaking to each other in Nepali. For a moment, they didn't see me, and I remained as still as could be, simply listening to them. Perhaps sensing someone nearby, they looked around and saw me.

We stared at each other for a moment, and I whispered, "*Namaste*, Auntie and Uncle. I speak Nepali, too."

"Good to meet you, little one. How old are you? Where did you live in Nepal?" They asked me many questions. I surprised myself by answering each one. Something about how they looked at me with such kindness, the fact that they spoke my language, and how I felt as we talked made me comfortable enough to share much of my story.

Their eyes grew teary when they heard how young I was. And they grew angry—I could see the fury flashing in their eyes—when I spoke of how I'd come to live here. They told me that they were in New Delhi to visit their daughter who had married the big *boss* of the brothel. "We don't like this place for our *chhori*. And we don't like it for you. We want to get you both out of here."

Their names were Mr. and Mrs. Janak. They took my hand and whispered, "Khushi, do you want to go back home to Nepal?" I stalled and stuttered, looking at the ground. I didn't know if I could believe them. *Sure, I had trusted them enough to tell them my story, but dare I trust them this much? Is this offer true—satya? Can they really help me?*

Mr. Janak, perhaps sensing my hesitation, pulled out his phone and showed me pictures. As he flipped through photo after photo of smiling, well-dressed children, he said, "Can you believe it, Khushi? These children are low-caste *Dalits*, just like you. Look at them. Look at how happy they are. They live in Kathmandu in a dormitory. They go to school. There is plenty of food, and it is safe. If you'd like, we can take you there."

They showed me pictures of three *Badi* girls and told me they were traveling around the world, sharing their stories. I scrunched my face in disbelief, marveling, *How in the world are they able to travel like this, to stand on stages and wear such beautiful clothes? Why are these large and small crowds listening to them?* I had never heard of a *Badi* being able to travel outside of Nepal, and here they were in photos in the United States. They looked so happy. They seemed so strong.

We heard someone coming, so we had to quickly end our conversation. Before he walked away, Mr. Janak said, "Khushi, think about this. But please don't tell anyone—not even our daughter—about our talk. I don't trust anyone here."

The next morning, Mr. Janak found me on the roof again and slipped me a little piece of paper with a map drawn on it and a phone number, saying, "Please, Khushi, please let us take you out of here. This is no place for a *keti* (girl). I'm worried what will happen to you if you stay. We are leaving for Kathmandu today, but we will not forget you. Call me at this number, and my wife and I will return for you. We will meet you at the place marked on this map. I promise, we will be there."

For days, I studied the map whenever I could, memorizing every street and the phone number. Then I threw the paper into the fire, destroying the evidence of my escape-dreams before someone else found it.

Although I didn't have a phone and had no way to call Mr. Janak, every day, I repeated his phone number to myself and pictured the map. Both became imprinted on my mind.

The periodic brothel raids continued. The *boss* instructed those of us who were young and underage to put on a burka during the raids, a garment that covers the whole body from head to toe and is worn by some Muslim women. When wearing a burka, the police did not—they could not—approach us. There were strict religious rules not to touch a woman wearing a burka. Even in the corrupt brothel, certain rules were followed. And the *bosses* knew it and used it to their advantage.

Three months passed. One night, as a regular *customer* was preparing to leave, I saw a cell phone in his pocket. With my heart beating through my chest, I asked him, "Please sir, may I use your phone for a short phone call?"

Surveying me for a brief moment, he paused, then handed me the phone. I quickly dialed Mr. Janak's number, hoping to the gods that he would answer. When he did, I whispered, "Mr. Janak, it's me, Khushi." I could hear the excitement in his voice as he asked me if I was ready. I took a deep breath, and I said, "*Ho*, Mr. Janak. Yes."

He didn't waste any time and spoke quickly. "Okay, Khushi, listen carefully. I know we can't talk long. Meet us at the spot I marked on the map in two days at four in the afternoon. Mrs. Janak and I will be there, I promise."

I went to bed that night and the next with trepidation and excitement.

I was ready to try to run one more time.

The morning of the second day, I went to the closet where the burkas were stashed for us younger girls to wear during raids. I curled it up into a ball and put it under my *sari* skirt. I walked up to the roof, then down to the street-side restaurant, looking behind me as I went. It was risky, and I couldn't believe that no one had followed me. Stepping out into the street, and once safely out of sight from the brothel, I put on the burka and ran for my life.

Remembering the map, I turned right at the *chiya* stand, left at the tall hotel, and ten minutes later, I found the spot marked on the map. Mr. and Mrs. Janak were there, just as they had promised!

They ran toward me and hugged me. I collapsed into them, partly in fear and partly in fatigue from my run, and they led me quickly to their car. As the car sped away toward the airport, and as tired as I was, I began to feel relieved and almost happy. *Is this a dream or am I truly free?*

But as we boarded the plane, I grew nervous. Terrified, in fact. It wasn't that I was scared to be on an airplane for the first time, nor was I worried I would be captured and forced to return to the brothel. I worried about what would happen if I made it home. *What will people think about me? Was the* ma'am *right? Have I brought shame on my family? Will any man ever want me after all I've done?*

As anxiety made my head hurt and tied my stomach up in painful knots, I fell in and out of fitful sleep, with my head on Mrs. Janak's shoulder. The thump of the plane's wheels startled me awake as we touched down in Kathmandu. No doubt seeing the nervousness in my eyes, Mrs. Janak gave me a reassuring hug and said, "Okay, dear Khushi, let's go meet the people who helped make your rescue possible. They are so excited to welcome you to Kathmandu."

Hannah (Part Three):
Global History Maker

Hannah's Story of Meeting Khushi

After meeting Khushi for the first time on the roof of the brothel on G.B. Road, Mr. and Mrs. Janak came to our organization's offices immediately when they returned to Kathmandu. After telling us her story, Mr. Janak spoke, "We are worried about her. She is so little, weak, and sick. We must go back for Khushi if she calls. Will you help us?"

They proposed this to us in 2017, after the five successful rescues of Puja and Gita, Meena's daughters and son, Meena, and the twenty-one children. We were as committed as ever to do what we could to free girls who were enslaved. We told them yes and began preparing immediately so that we would be ready if and when she called.

When Mr. and Mrs. Janak got the phone call from Khushi, all of us—our organization's fifty staff and 680 children who now lived in the dormitories in Kathmandu—began hoping and praying that Khushi would soon be safely in our care. As Mr. and Mrs. Janak returned to New Delhi for her rescue, we knew that it was tremendously dangerous ... for them and for Khushi.

For several days, it seemed that these three were all anyone thought or talked about. So, when Mr. and Mrs. Janak called us, ecstatic with the good news that Khushi was safely in their care and they were about to board their flight bound for Kathmandu, we breathed a huge sigh of collective relief.

When I heard she had landed and was heading to our office, I hopped on my scooter right after school and rode as fast as I could to meet and welcome her. I ran up the flights of stairs, jumping up two stairs at a time, my heart racing as I leapt.

I burst into the room where Khushi was sitting, and when I saw her, I could not believe it. She was even smaller than I imagined, *so little* to have been through *so much*. I walked up to her and gave her a big hug, saying, "Khushi, welcome. We are so happy you are here. You are safe now, and you can stay as long as you'd like."

She nodded wearily, with a hint of a smile on her little lips. As I looked at her, I was moved by the miracle of her life. I wanted to protect her from any more pain. First things first, though, I needed to get Khushi comfortable in her new dormitory. I took her hand, saying, "Come with me, Khushi, you have traveled long and far. You must be tired and hungry. Let's go meet the other girls. They are so excited to see you!"

When we walked into one of our seven dormitories in Kathmandu, right away, there was a surprise waiting for her. Entering the ground floor kitchen, the housemother was preparing a delicious meal of *dal bhat* (lentils and rice) with chicken, an extra special treat. "Khushi," she said, "we don't have meat every day, but today, do you know why we are having this special meal and celebrating?" Khushi shook her head, so our housemother continued. "Dearest *keti*, we are celebrating your return sweet girl, your life today, and your bright future."

I took Khushi's hand and looked her in the eyes, saying, *"Ho,* just like that, Khushi. Yes, you've moved from a future that once looked hopeless and dark to a new, bright one. And no one can stand between you and this future full of freedom and possibility.

It's true. *Satya*."

I asked, "Do you want to check out your bedroom and meet some of the other girls?" She nodded her answer, and we headed upstairs. On top of her bed that had been made with fresh-smelling, clean sheets sat a new set of clean clothes and her school uniform. When she asked me what the uniform was for, I told her, "Khushi, do you remember what Mr. and Mrs. Janak told you about our school? You can go to school as soon as you want. If you need some time, you can take it … or you can begin tomorrow."

She looked at me in stunned silence. Then, after taking a warm shower, she put on her clean clothes, enjoyed a nourishing meal, and fell into bed at the end of the day. As I went to tell her goodnight, I found she had already fallen asleep. How peacefully my beloved *bahini*—my beloved little sister—looked as she slept that first night with us. Gazing at her teeny face in great gratitude, I kissed her on the cheek.

Some girls take days, weeks, and months to be ready to go to school after being rescued from or escaping the brothels. The trauma they have experienced is often so great that they cannot fully welcome and embrace this new season of life. But Khushi was ready to begin right away. The next morning, when she came to breakfast, she stood proud and tall in her school uniform. As she sipped her *chiya*, her eyes had a bit of a sparkle in them as she silently sat amid a circle of chattering girls.

A few days later, when I asked Khushi about school and how she was feeling, she spoke honestly. "Hannah, I'm worried. I've not talked much to anyone because I'm nervous that if the girls hear my whole story, they will reject me. I've been in a bad place and done such bad things."

I hugged her and told her that many of these girls had difficult stories too. "Khushi, when you are ready, you can share your true story—your *satya* story—the whole thing. Trust me. There is nothing that we've not heard. When girls get the courage to speak their true story, time after time, they say they feel lighter. It is often the spark that starts their healing. But there's no need to rush. You are safe and loved, now, whether or not you choose to ever tell your story." I told her that we'd be ready to listen whenever she was ready to speak.

And, eventually, tell us she did. *Bistarai,* she slowly told us her story. As she did, we all encouraged her. We loved her. We, too, told her our hard and painful stories. As often was the case, when one girl cried, every girl cried. Each of us had experienced pain and hardship. We talked about the ways we had been healed and the ways in which we still ached.

After a month with us, Khushi made the trip back to the far west of Nepal to see her *aama* for the first time since her rescue. She had been gone for more than a year. Her mom didn't have a phone, so Khushi had not been able to call her to tell her she was okay.

When her mom opened the door, she squealed with surprise. Ushering her into the house, she told Khushi that she could not believe her eyes that she was alive. "After you were gone for one year, I gave up hope of ever seeing you again, *chhori.* When you didn't return from the market, do you know what I thought? I worried that you had been murdered. I never did feel good about you leaving the house by yourself—there is so much danger outside our doors in Bardiya. But I can barely believe it. You are home, my daughter. What a dream come true!"

After her mom made some *chiya,* Khushi shared her story from beginning to end. Her mom was speechless and kept looking at her daughter with awe. But when she was finished, and her mom gave her another hug and kiss, Khushi's throat tightened in fear. As her mom looked at her, Khushi saw something in her eyes and wondered, *Is she ashamed of me? What does she think of me now?*

Hesitating, Khushi asked, "Mom, what is it? What are you thinking?"

Her *aama* replied, "Khushi, I'm so glad you are home, but to be honest, I am afraid. What man will ever want to marry you with this background? What kind of future do you have?"

Khushi told her mom about going to school in Kathmandu and the friends she had made in just a month. "Mom, they promise me that I have a good future—and I believe them. Watch and you'll see. I don't want to miss this opportunity—I need to go back to Kathmandu and continue my studies." Her mom nodded her agreement, and the next morning, Khushi got on a bus and returned to Kathmandu.

When she told me about her talk with her mom, Khushi wept. She had put on a brave face for her mom, but underneath, the very same worries about her future had been burdening her heart. Hearing her *aama* speak them out loud made them seem even more real. I listened. I cried with her. I begged her to keep talking with her sisters and me and assured her that we would, together, make our way through the struggles.

As the weeks passed, she kept doing better and better. When I asked her about it, she smiled and told me, "I just feel happier. Hannah *didi*, I know I'm lucky to be able to go to school and to be surrounded by my new family of sisters here. Sister, I actually think I'm starting to believe for myself that I *do* have a bright future." We sat quietly together for a moment and then gave each other a big hug. She then ran off to her next class, with a skip in her step.

There Is Much More to Do!

I found myself captivated by the memories of the many miraculous rescues and escapes of those I loved. Awe and joy filled my heart as I looked around and saw them living with freedom and security.

But amid a heart full of gratitude, I felt a fire blazing in my stomach. I was not at rest. Many days, I was more angry than cheerful as I thought about how many were *still* enslaved. So many women and girls were *still* in brothels, being abused by men and *ma'ams*. I would keep fighting for them too.

Yes, there is much more to do.

Why?!

I have heard it said by more than one government official that "The *Badi* just don't want our help."

This is not true. Oh no—far from it. While I can't speak for all *Badi*, I can speak for myself and many *Badi* whose desires and dreams I know well.

This is what I would like to say today to the government of Nepal: *Why* do you not stand up for us? *Why* do you stand by? *Why* do you blame us?

We need a lot, but we don't need what you think. We are not looking for handouts or for you to tell us what to do. The leadership must come from within our own people, not from the outside. We need a little bit of support, and we will do the rest.

We need access for *Badi* youth to be educated. Right now, our children cannot go to school. Even though caste is illegal, they are kicked out because of their *Badi* name. Yet, without education, change will not come.

We need the crime of human trafficking to be enforced with police protection and follow-through. Traffickers must go to jail and be fined. When fines are imposed, *Badi* vocational training livelihood programs could be funded.

We need to be able to own our land. We have been landless for too long. Many of our people are still living in the jungle, surrounded by wild animals, and lack shelter from the summer's oppressive heat and winter's bone-chilling temperatures.

We need the dignity of citizenship. While I appreciate that the government now grants the status of citizenship to *Badi* people today, most *Badi* do not have birth certificates. Without birth certificates, our people cannot travel, get government jobs, or enlist in the army. Lacking proof of identity, most doors of opportunity stay firmly shut.

The status of our people must rise. The *Badi* can and must rise out of *the dust of Nepal*. But we don't need outsiders to do the work *for* us. We just need a few people to listen, to support what we are already doing, and do the work *with* us.

It's Much Better Today, But ...

Today, my life is a lot better—infinitely better than most *Badi* have experienced for many generations. I live in an apartment in a very nice part of the city. I have had an unparalleled education and incredible opportunities. I can travel the world. It took patience and tenacity, but in 2012, I was able to obtain my citizenship, and in 2013, my passport—a rarity for a *Badi* in Nepal. My future is bright. I am grateful beyond measure.

However, amid all the great aspects of my story, still today, I experience caste discrimination. Several years ago on my college campus, before my classmates knew I was *Badi*, they would walk and talk with me. But the moment they heard I was *Badi*, they began to exclude and insult me. They no longer wanted anything to do with me and looked at me with distaste, saying, "You, Hannah Badi, pollute our campus. You do not belong here with us."

Even now, in legal matters, my name impacts my freedom and my choices. In 2017, I went to our government offices to obtain a travel visa. The official looked over his glasses at me, as the hatred and disdain he felt were made clear in his gaze and words. "It looks like you have traveled to many places: Australia, throughout Asia, the US, and Europe. How is it that you, a *Badi*, are traveling like this?" He narrowed his eyes and looked at me with disgust. "Something is not right here." Although he reluctantly issued my travel visa, I walked out of his office discouraged and angry. *How long will I be treated this way? Just because of my* Badi *name and* untouchable *caste?*

Later in the year, I was invited to be a keynote speaker at a gala in the United States. The moment I finished my speech, the crowd erupted in cheers and rose to their feet. As I stood in awe, minutes after receiving my first standing ovation, the president of a university approached me with tears in his eyes, saying, "Hannah, we would like to offer you a four-year scholarship to our college. It would be a great privilege for our faculty and students to have you as part of our school."

A scholarship to a university in the United States?! I was dizzy with excitement and thankfulness, immediately responding with an enthusiastic "Yes!" I planned to begin in the fall of 2018. As I prepared for this opportunity, I stayed with some friends in Florida and took a six-month English intensive course. I wanted to make sure that when I went to college, I had more fluency and was comfortable reading and speaking English.

I returned to Nepal in spring 2018 to apply for my student visa. Stepping into the embassy office, I was, once again, face-to-face with the same man who treated me contemptuously the last time I applied.

"Hannah *Ba ... di.*" He said my last name slowly and with a frown. "I remember you. No, you cannot go to the United States to study. I'm not going to approve your request for a student visa. There is no way you have enough money or abilities for this request to be legitimate. This is an impossibility."

Frustrated but undeterred, I was prepared for this. I cleared my throat, took a breath, and asked him to look at two items in my application file. I had included my acceptance letter from the college, with evidence that I'd received a fully paid college scholarship for four years, along with documentation from the family who offered to host me at their home, rent-free, throughout my four years of study. As he flipped each page over, I watched his brow become furrowed and his frown more pronounced. I found myself lamenting, *How long will I need to prove myself to men like him? This is not right, not fair! Someday, I dream that my name will no longer narrowly define what I can or cannot do.*

He shuffled through the paperwork and finally glared at me over his glasses with suspicion. "I still don't believe you. There is no way, no reason, that a college would want *you*. Why in the world would they ever choose *you*, a *Badi*? This is a scam." Irritated, he grabbed a stamp and slammed his answer—"Denied"—on my visa application.

My application was accurate and 100 percent true—*satya*. Although there was nothing false or made up in it, not one word, it did not matter. Once again, my dreams were denied for one reason: because of my *Badi* name.

I was determined not to allow his denial and disregard to stop me. It wasn't easy, but I fought with all my heart. I tried two more times and spent countless hours to secure the extra documentation needed to prove my case. Finally, I received my student visa from a different official. I was one step closer to my dream of going to college, but my goodness ... it was not easy!

Propelled to Fly

Some days, when I consider the ugly and recycled stories of how the *Badi* have been treated—over and over, for hundreds and hundreds of years—and how we have treated one another, I am incensed.

There are days that I feel I might burn up from my anger.

Our *Badi* girls *are* beautiful. *So what?* That doesn't mean they should be forced to sell their bodies for the profit and pleasure of men.

I love music and dancing. *So what?* That doesn't mean that I am dancing for sex or that men are free to touch my body as they wish.

I have been judged since the time I was born for things I cannot control: my last name, my skin color, my gender, and my socioeconomic status. Far too often, people have treated me as less than human ... as if I do not matter.

I, too, am a human being.

I, too, have red blood coursing through my veins.

For much of my life, I have been rejected, laughed at, and despised because I am *Badi*. Those with a more important last name, more money, or a seemingly better reputation have looked down on me. I have been at the bottom of the heap for too long, and I am tired of the sting of these looks of condescension.

I have been judged for the opportunities I have been given as if they should not have been offered to me. Yes, I have had an excellent education. *Ho*, I get to travel around the world. What makes me the angriest is when people are shocked or offended to see me, "a *Badi* girl," having these privileges ... as if my name should make these opportunities impossible. I will not cower with shame but will instead stand with pride and gratitude.

Now I know—with everything in me—that no one has the right to judge and mock me for who I am. It has taken me some time and tenacity to get here, but I see how this pain propelled me to fly. Although many have tried to cut my wings, they were not able to stop me. In fact, their opposition and mistreatment made me stronger. I am now soaring high like an eagle.

People from my village—even my own family members—have tried to silence and intimidate me to stop flying and fighting. Many have told me that it is useless to try to change anything, saying, "If this is our fate, why try to change it? Our destiny is already set, and the problems are too big for anyone to fix. Who do you think you are, Hannah?"

Still today, many believe this way. Not me. We must do what we can, together, to change what is broken, to share hope, and to fight for freedom for those who are suffering. I will not stop sharing and shouting this message to my people and to the world. It is my destiny. It is my calling. It is my warrior cry.

Freed by Forgiveness

A few years ago, I went home to visit my mom and dad. Walking through the village one morning, I saw my cousin, a well-known trafficker in our village. Without giving it much thought, I marched right up to him and furiously shouted into his face, "How can you do this to our people? Do you not have a heart? People are not property. We are not animals. Girls are not for you to buy and sell, to take from their homes!"

He looked nervous. Not even looking at me, he kept his eyes lowered to the ground. A crowd had begun to form around us. I was not finished, so I kept ranting, "They are human beings, just like you. Too many of my sisters have been trafficked, and I wonder ... was it *you* who sold them? Cousin, do you not hear their screams?"

I was on fire with fury.

His impassioned response and pained look in his eyes stopped my tirade in an instant. "Hannah, please. You don't understand. I, too, am human and have a heart. You asked if I hear their screams. No, I don't. I don't hear their screams, not because I don't care but because the rumbling of my stomach is louder. This is the truth, I promise."

I grew quiet.

In that moment, something softened in me as the anger and judgment dissipated. As I looked at him, I now saw emptiness and pain. I saw desperation.

That day, he taught me something I will never forget. Make no mistake, I was not about to excuse his actions or deny the undeniable agony he caused others. But while I saw a deeply flawed human being who furthered a system that was fundamentally unjust, I also saw my cousin and understood human trafficking in a new light.

A seed was planted that day, and I now carry a deeper sense of understanding and love for people like my cousin—that those who make the choice to hurt others are themselves hurting. I gained a keen sense that for a father to sell his daughter, that father must himself be deeply despairing and hopeless. My eyes were opened to see a problem that was more complex than I had ever imagined.

I have had much to learn … and much to forgive.

I have chosen to forgive more often and more deeply. *Bistarai*, I have come to believe that no one is ultimately unforgivable. Slowly, I've come to trust that no one is beyond the reach of redemption.

I've seen it to be true—over and over. Ram, the man who sold Meena to the tractor brothers, is now an elder and respected spiritual leader in our village. He now takes special care of my parents and treats them with immeasurable respect. He is one of the great champions of girls and keeps a watchful eye on those he believes are a part of the dark web of trafficking. More than anything, I see a fierce love for people in him that makes our village more safe and secure.

The cousin who taught me the invaluable lesson of the complexities of human trafficking is trying to break away from the family business of brothels and trafficking. Time will tell if he will be able to move into a way of life that is free and good.

My heart has even softened toward Chaha, the pimp who trafficked my sisters and best friends. I feel more sorrow for her than anger today. Her life is in shambles. It is very much broken. I don't know the details, but because of owing money to a brothel *boss*, she is not able to return to India. She has become destitute. The last time I saw her in the village, she looked so forlorn. As I walked past her and greeted her, she mumbled her response, "*Namaste*," and didn't look at me. She has lost everything. Power … gone. Money … gone. Freedom … gone.

Today, I am *with* my cousin and Chaha—not against them—as they make their way. I have a fervent hope that they will turn around and become people who help others instead of hurting them. I do not say this lightly—for they have caused much injury to those I love.

I will fight injustice with everything in me, yes. But the experience with my cousin helped me learn that I need to keep a watchful eye on myself as I fight. I am aware of my tendency to become shackled by resentment. If I am not careful, it will form a tight and oppressive grip that won't let me go—and I will be less able to do the work to which I have been called. Thus, I choose to forgive often. Otherwise, I believe my anger would have burned me up by now. It is true—*satya*—I'm sure of it.

But make no mistake, I am not stopping.

Now I am simply freer to fight.

The Real Hero

I promised to tell my 100 percent true—*satya*—story. But this two-part truth-telling tale is not easy for me to share.

Part 1. There was a day that I nearly broke under the weight of all that I was carrying in life—all I wanted, hoped, and dreamed of for the future, the suffering of so many in my community, the stories of my sisters and the women I wanted to help still enslaved in the brothels.

Life became too heavy and hard.

When I was nineteen, I tried to commit suicide.

I tried to kill myself by swallowing an entire bottle of pills. I wanted to wake up in heaven, but when I awoke, I found myself in the hospital.

Until that moment, I hadn't realized just how much pain I was in. I began to acknowledge—for the first time—the depths of trauma in my life. Even though I was living in an incredibly supportive community, and I had so much for which to be thankful, I hid parts of my pain, even from my most trusted friends. I needed to learn and practice being more honest with a trusted few about how much I was hurting.

Part 2. I need to be 100 percent honest with you too. I am not only an often-despised minority when it comes to my *Badi* name, but also when it comes to my faith. In Nepal, as of 2019, the religions were broken down as follows: 81 percent of the population is Hindu, 9 percent are Buddhist, 4 percent are Muslim, and 1 percent is Christian. Each of the storytellers—as am I—is a Christian, one of the religious minorities in Nepal.

May I keep sharing my 100 percent true—*satya*—story with you? I cannot tell my story fully without speaking about my connection to Jesus and of the deep roots of my faith as a Christian. Even if—especially if—you are from a different religious tradition than me, I hope you believe, as I do, that we can still be deeply connected and stay connected. I believe that we are all one family ... and that we belong to each other, amid whatever differences exist between us.

I know, without a shadow of a doubt, that Jesus is the reason I am alive today. Jesus removed the pain from my heart and was the primary source of my healing in the days following my suicide attempt.

As grateful as I am to my family and supportive community around the world, it is not these people for whom I am most thankful. My life has been most changed because of the great love of Jesus. It is His love that strengthens my faith, fueling me to be the fierce warrior of justice that I am today. Jesus is the One who gives me courage to fight for and rescue girls from brothels and sustains my energy to protect thousands more from ever being trafficked.

Yes, Jesus is the real Hero. Whenever I get a chance, I want to shout from the rooftops what He has done for me. I wholly believe— as do each of the other four storytellers in this story—that we are healed *first* by Him and *then* by people ... not the other way around.

Jesus is the ultimate Warrior fighting for me. I am happy doing what I can to be part of His warrior work. I have seen miracle after miracle of what I know has only been done because of His presence and love for all people.

Many people say to my sisters and me, "Your God, Jesus, is only for *Dalit* people." While I don't believe He is *only* for *Dalits*, I do understand why we *Dalits* love Him. The love and acceptance we feel from Him is a warmth we do not often feel as *untouchables*. Yes, His love makes each of us feel we are important and valuable.

Caste is a broken mindset, and I believe the only solution for this wrecked system is Jesus. The changes that need to be made are too great to accomplish without Him. Jesus loves all people equally and extravagantly. In His eyes, there is no caste system. He doesn't love one person more than another. We need not do anything to elevate our status or our name in His eyes. Jesus loves us more than we will ever understand.

And so, day by day, I fall more in love with Jesus. When I feel His love, it matters less to me what people say about me, and the pain in my life is lessened. The truest thing I know is this: Nothing and no one can stand in the way of His love for me and His good plan for my life. Jesus plants bigger and better dreams in my heart than I could ever imagine—and He is the One who makes them come true.

A Big Dream

I am the first girl to go to high school and college from my village, but I am not stopping now. I want to finish university, rescue more girls, and educate my people and the world about what is possible to change—together.

Bidhya Devi Bhandari was elected president in 2015. She is the first female head of state in our country. She inspires me. She makes me think, *If she can do it, so can I.*

My big dream is to be the first *Dalit* woman prime minister in the history of Nepal, in part because I want to show the world—and my people—that we are *no longer untouchable.*

But for now, I am deeply at peace and content to be taking one step and one leap at a time—and, being true to my *Badi* name, whirling my way as I go.

Not the End

Sangeeta: Mother to Many

When Given the Choice, Why Return?

love my work with Hannah in our community organization in Nepal. It is a family endeavor. My brother, Raju, started the organization, and one by one, every member of our family has become a part of it in some way. I spend my days in our halfway house and in our dormitories with girls and women who have been rescued or experienced trauma before they came to us.

When people hear what I do, they often ask me:

"Why do girls return to the brothels once they're free? It doesn't make sense that they'd ever go back."

"If given the choice, why do they not leave?"

"Is there really a time when they are free to return home from the brothels?"

Yes, it's true—*satya*—that once a girl has paid off her purchase price, she is often free to leave the brothel. To those who are free and have never known someone who has lived in an environment like a brothel, it's hard to grasp why they would ever stay, if given the chance to leave.

It's all very complicated, but I will speak to what I have come to understand. Whether born in a brothel or trafficked to a brothel as a young girl, these girls are brainwashed. They are indoctrinated with messages that there is nothing better for them in the world beyond the brothel and no one else wants them. Their very sense of self is obliterated. It is pounded to dust. They are told by pimps and *ma'ams* things like:

"You are just like the stinking garbage outside the brothel."

"No man will ever want you after having sex with thousands of others."

"You are worthless and have brought shame to your family, and they never want to see you again."

In this distorted world, people are seen as property. Power is palpable. Those at the top stop at nothing to abuse, coerce, and kill to protect what they believe belongs to them. From the moment they arrive, these girls are serially raped and forced to use drugs and alcohol. I have never been anywhere that feels as oppressive as G.B. Road in New Delhi, where our storytellers were trafficked. Day and night, girls peek out of barred windows. I know it from talking to these girls when they come back from G.B. Road: behind those bars, unimaginable terror and daily torture is the way of life. Garbage piles, small and large, are everywhere, trash is always underfoot, and men urinate in the alleys. The smells are so strong and putrid, and the sense of oppression so thick, that I am overcome. Often, I gag or vomit as I walk down the streets of G.B. Road.

People come to this red-light district from all over the world. Minds have been twisted and hearts distorted to believe it is in the realm of reason to buy and sell, to use and abuse, these young and very vulnerable girls.

Moving Into a Life of Freedom

After a rescued girl first comes to us, we keep her very busy. A free life can be hard to adjust to and embrace. Thus, we try to engage each one in good, interesting, and joyful work that creates a sense of connection and community with others.

Many girls come to us addicted to alcohol and drugs. These were part of their lives: often first forced, then normalized, and then part of how they coped with the horrors of life in a brothel. When a girl comes to us, we do not tell her to stop smoking or drinking right away. We create an environment of healing, yes—but we trust, and we move *bistarai, bistarai*. Slowly, slowly.

We follow their lead and give them as many choices as we can. Even in little things like what to eat, what time to get up and go to bed, and what to do with their free time. Having been forced and disempowered for so long, it is time for them to learn how to make choices.

These girls have often lived for so many years without meaning. We offer opportunities for them to feed their lives with peace and purpose. Dancing makes many of them feel free, so I often turn on music. In the world, the best singers and dancers are *Badi*. So, in terms of "dance therapy," it is not complicated. In fact, it is simple. They just need a chance to dance what's inside. It is in their blood.

When they dance, I am their audience. When they decide it is time to share their story, I listen. When they are listened to, heaviness falls away from them. When they cry, I cry. I hug them whenever I can.

What I do from the very start is *love* them. Love is the most important ingredient. Love is what heals, what creates hope, what sets them up with a good future. I understand that there will be times when they will be aggressive and bitter—they have been through unspeakable horrors. I let them feel those feelings and love them through it all.

Facing the Giants

When it comes to their complete and whole healing, like Hannah, I cannot tell this story without talking about Jesus. Because when He touches them and heals their hearts, the broken parts fall away. Each time. Sometimes it happens in massive and miraculous ways, in the blink of an eye. At other times, it happens little by little and day by day ... *bistarai*. Slowly.

Have you heard the story of David and Goliath? This is a picture of how I see my work. The young boy David defeats the giant Goliath with a little stone. This tale is about the powerless overcoming the powerful, about holding onto hope, even when faced with insurmountable odds. This story is my heartbeat and prayer for my life with these girls.

For me, the "little stone" is many things. It is prayer. It is my faith in Jesus. It is my trust that He has a big love for these girls. It is my belief that He will help and empower our organization to rescue and heal these broken girls.

But do you know what? The rescuing is the simple and easy part, really. When they come to us, we are like a healing pool. Yes, we give them lots of therapy, good food, education, and shelter. But without Jesus, the healing only goes so far. Without Him, I don't believe they can wholly heal their wounds. It's true; too much pain has been inflicted without a miracle to start over again.

This happened with Sakhira. After being electrocuted by the police who rescued her from the brothel, her body was not the only thing that was scarred. It seemed she might have experienced just too much trauma to ever be well again. When she first came to Kathmandu, I gave her lots of hugs and told her hundreds of times, "Sakhira, I love you ... we all love you." Sure, it helped a little to feel my love as an auntie. But I remember the day that everything changed. When she felt the love of God—the love of Jesus—something happened, and her deepest wounds were healed. Right away, she smiled more often, and she began to dance and sing again. Some days, it almost seemed like her face would glow with peace and happiness.

So, for me, the darker the day, the more I pray. When I talk with these girls, when I hear and feel their pain, when I see the scars on their bodies from being beaten and burned, I pray. I pray every day. I must. And when I go into the hellhole of G.B. Road, I pray with each step. I do not stop praying. I cannot stop. I am not that brave. I need supernatural support and strength. I need more light than I have within me.

My daily prayer is this: "Give me strength. May Your Light be greater than the darkness."

My Healed and Happy Heart
(As Shared by Meena)

When I first returned to Nepal, my body was broken and so was my spirit. I did not think I could ever be healthy or happy again. But many encouraged me each day. Love surrounded me, and *bistarai*, this community has slowly helped me heal.

Sangeeta Auntie was a big part of my life when I first came back. She was kind, safe, good, and fierce in her love. Sangeeta did so many things to encourage me and make me happy. I remember when she learned that I loved to eat meat, she often brought steaming platters of food with extra meat in it, just for me. I hadn't eaten like that for so long, longer than I could remember. Other days, she'd surprise me with a bag of nice clothes. She'd say, "These clothes are just to remind you how special and loved you are, Meena."

Sangeeta Auntie would tell me all the time, "I love you. God has a plan for you. A good plan. Don't give up." *Bistarai*, slowly, I began to dream again. Now, my big dream is to buy my parents a nice house with a comfortable bed and plenty of food to eat. I do not want them to be hungry ever again. Their lives have been hard, and they have given so much to try to make it better for my sisters and me.

I know it. I'm lucky to be here, happy to be free. But to be honest, there are still days when I wake up and feel sad … sometimes I cannot shake it for days and days. When this happens, it seems like the light has gone from the world, and my friends tell me that they don't know how to connect with me or help me. Sometimes, without warning, my body will start to shake or I will have a seizure. Other times, I have a hard time breathing, gripped by fear and memories from my days in the brothels.

Sangeeta says this is called "post-traumatic stress" from the years with the tractor men and on G.B. Road. "*Bistarai, bistarai,* Meena," she tells me. "Slowly, slowly, you'll get better, grow stronger, and be happier. It just takes time. We're with you." I feel their support. And I feel the support and love of Jesus. When I sing and pray, I feel free and believe that I can make it one more day. I cannot imagine trying to live this life without His love and presence. It would be just too hard and hopeless. Hannah tells me all the time that she has never seen anyone sing and worship Jesus the way I do. I tell her, "I don't think anyone has as much reason to sing and worship as I do!" It's true. *Satya.*

Each day, as I hug and kiss my beautiful children, I cannot believe that we are safe and we are home. As I cuddle with them at the end of our day, it makes my heart happy. How happy they are each day at school and how they love their friends.

And, oh, how well they sing and dance!

After all, we are a *musical people.*

We are *Badi.*

Epilogue

The stories continue and are still unfolding. More history is to be made, and these are the ones making it.

Hannah received her student visa. Before she returned to the United States, she spoke with a group of high-level government officials in Nepal and shared her dream publicly to one day become prime minister, after which she received the second standing ovation of her life. She has not yet returned to the US to attend university and is now focusing on her work as CEO of Himalayan Entrepreneur Resources (HER) in Nepal.

Meena is now living in one of the most exclusive parts of Kathmandu, receiving vocational training and spending time with her children.

Khushi is now studying in Kathmandu. She spent a semester abroad in Singapore and Japan. Her dream is to become a world-famous dancer.

Aasha has a son and a daughter and loves her work at a prestigious school in Kathmandu. She and her husband are still saving to build a house on the land they've already purchased.

Sakhira left Nepal and moved back to India with the love of her life, Mahesh. She has a daughter and still dreams of finishing her high school education one day.

Hannah, Aasha, and Meena's mom and dad still live in the village of Jhuprakhola. They have both overcome major health challenges, and their three daughters are delighted to report that their parents are strong, healthy, and happy.

Bina, Meena's eldest daughter, is extremely intelligent, most recently receiving top marks on her school exams. She is the first *Badi* girl to study at one of Nepal's most esteemed schools, Xavier International College.

Kaya, Nanu, and Rahul, Meena's three youngest children, are in school; they love studying, singing, dancing, and playing all day long.

Gita married and went with her husband to the Middle East for a few years to work. They are now back in Nepal. She is receiving training to become a social worker and plans to focus on supporting the needs of the *Badi* community.

Puja is proud to be able to make enough money to provide for the needs of her family in Nepal.

References

Timeline

A note about dates and this timeline. One of the challenges among the *Badi* people and other ethnic groups in Nepal has been that they have been denied citizenship because sometimes children do not know who their father is. Furthermore, in Nepal, there has often not been a legal record of a child's birthdate. (Now, it is changing, due to educational requirements of citizenship.) In addition, the Nepali calendar—also known as "Bikram Sambat"—is approximately 56 years, 8 months ahead of the Gregorian/English/AD calendar. Thus, many people in Nepal do not know their exact date of birth. Accuracy with dates has been complex and difficult to keep straight.

1954   Caste made illegal in Nepal

1976   Hannah's mom (Maya) born

1988   Hannah's mom proposed to and then raped (12 years old)
        Meena born

1991   Aasha born

1995   Hannah born, although due to confusion over her birth
        year, some of her legal papers say that she was born in 1993

1996	Sakhira born
	Nepal Communist Party launches violent "people's war" (lasts 10 years)
1997	Meena sold to tractor brothers in India (9 years old)
1999	Meena (11 years old) gives birth to son (Anas)
2000	Meena (12 years old) gives birth to daughter (Bina) / returns to Nepal with children / Anas abducted and taken back to India
2002	Meena sold to brothel in India (14 years old)
2003	Khushi born
	Hannah forced to carry bombs by Maoists (8 years old)
	Aasha forced to marry / trafficked to India (12 years old)
	Gita and Puja trafficked to India
2004	Hannah gets sick and sexually assaulted by doctor (9 years old)
2005	Aasha runs away from brothel / forced to retrieve bomb (14 years old)
2006	Aasha falls in love and gets married (15 years old)
	Sakhira moves to Hannah's village (10 years old)
2007	Sakhira assaulted by her sister's husband & trafficked to India (11 years old)
	Meena deemed "work old" / moved from G.B. Road to Meerut (19 years old)
2008	Monarchy in Nepal ends
	Meena's daughter (Kaya) born

2009   Hannah meets Raju and Håkan / moves to Kathmandu, along with 33 *Badi* girls (14 years old)

Sakhira's "rescue" and abuse by police (13 years old)

Meena's daughter (Nanu) born; Aasha's daughter (Preeti) born

2010   Hannah's sickness is gone (15 years old)

Gita and Puja return to Nepal / tell Hannah that Meena is alive

2011   Gita and Puja rescued

Aasha's son (Suraj) born

2012   Meena's daughters (Kaya and Nanu) rescued / Preeti (Aasha's daughter) taken to Kathmandu

2013   Aasha goes to Kuwait for work (22 years old)

2014   Meena's son, Rahul, born and rescued

Hannah attempts suicide (19 years old)

2015   Aasha returns to Nepal from Kuwait (24 years old)

Hannah fights for Jiya in the village / followed and beaten up in Kathmandu / goes on international tour (20 years old)

Sarah asked to write *No Longer Untouchable* book

Meena rescued (27 years old)

2016   Meena badly beaten up by boyfriend (Rajesh)

Sarah goes to Nepal to do research for *No Longer Untouchable*

Twenty-one children rescued from Anand Vihar, India

Sakhira leaves Nepal for India to visit her mom and gets married (20 years old)

Khushi trafficked from Nepal to India (13 years old)

2017   Khushi rescued (14 years old)

Sarah and storytellers begin to craft *No Longer Untouchable*

Hannah is offered a full-ride scholarship at a US university

2018   Aasha makes history and buys land in Kathmandu (27 years old)

Hannah is first denied and then succeeds in obtaining her student visa so she can return to the US for university

2020   Hannah becomes CEO of Himalayan Entrepreneur Resources (HER)

Glossary of Terms

Due to the proximity of Nepal and India, Nepali and Hindi share some similarities. Additionally, both languages originated from the Sanskrit. If a word is Nepali, we have noted it with **. If a word is Hindi, we have noted it with *. If the word is both Nepali and Hindi, we have not included a mark.

A
aama mom
amala gooseberries

B
bachchaharu children
bahini/bahiniharu little sister/little sisters, also used to refer to others in one's generation
badar monkey
bhai little brother, also used to refer to others in one's generation
bistarai a process of doing things slowly over time
Bollywood the Indian movie industry
buba dad

C
**chiya spiced tea prepared with tea leaves, spices, milk, and sugar
**chiyawalharu / *chaiwallahs tea sellers
chaat fried dough topped with potatoes, chickpeas, and yogurt
**chhora son
**chhori daughter
**chituwa leopard

D
**dal bhat lentils and rice
**dai elder brother, also used to refer to others in one's generation
didi elder sister, also used to refer to others in one's generation

H
**hajuraama grandmother
**hajurbuba grandfather
Hindi the official language of Northern India
**ho yes
**hunchha okay/yes

J
**Jaimasi common greeting among Christians meaning, "victory to the Messiah"

K
**kaka uncle or older man
**keti girl
Khamsi the language of the Badi
**kitab book
**kukur dog
kurta a long and loose shirt, common in Nepal and India

M
madal a Nepali drum
machcharaharu mosquitoes
marriage among some ethnic groups in Nepal—and in the families of our storytellers—when a person says they are "married," it does not always mean that there has been a marriage ceremony or that there is a legal "marriage certificate." If people live together, they often refer to one another as "husband" or "wife," and others refer to them as "married."

N
Namaste common greeting in Nepal and India meaning, "I bless the divine in you"

P
paan a folded leaf that is filled with nut, lime, and tobacco that is often spat out after being chewed
paratha a flat, thick piece of fried bread

R
rakshi homemade liquor
rupee Nepali and Indian currency

S
sari a typical garment worn by women; long piece of fabric wrapped around the body
sasu mother-in-law
satya true
swasni a casual/slang word for wife, used when a relationship is difficult or unhappy

T
thalis full plates of food

Calls to Inspired ACTion

The darkness is great, and the struggles are oh so very real. So are the light-bearers, the warriors of love and justice.

Human Trafficking Toolkit

Go to <u>SeedsOfExchange.org/HumanTraffickingToolkit</u> for a helpful resource and to connect with people and organizations we know, treasure, and respect who are fighting against human trafficking. As you explore, consider how you are inspired to act. Personally connect with these folks and give, volunteer, and travel. Get ready to feel good as you do good.

Join the Seeds Community

If you've ever wondered how one person could possibly make a difference just by showing up exactly as they are—welcome to the Seeds of Exchange community.

Seeds of Exchange creates good in the world through inspiring people to make a local and global difference—together. Through building community, sharing stories, and encouraging ways to tangibly care for each other, this is a place to go if you want to make an indelible dent in global human rights and in the day-to-day lives of those nearest and dearest to you.

We are committed to serve, love, respond to, collaborate with, and make a real difference in the daily lives of each other. Not merely with *ideas or talk*, but in action, in waking people up to their vital part in this work. We are mobilizers and master connectors of many (individuals, nonprofits, government agencies, or businesses), everyday philanthropists who believe everyone has something of value to give, and storytellers who amplify the tales of the good being done and the darkness present that still need to be flooded with light.

Together, we talk about and do stuff that matters: restore justice, evoke dignity, provide shelter, share food with the hungry, demand and increase fair practices in the workplace, eliminate poverty, transform lives with education, protect children, offer micro-loans, fuel small and mighty grassroots organizations, give generously and humbly share what we can with those who have little, facilitate conversations between those who are divided and at odds, celebrate and respect people who are "different" from us, serve those closest to us with love (family, friends, neighbors), and take time to be still through practicing regular rhythms of soul care.

No one person does all of this. We each have been destined to do work in ways that we cannot do alone. Step by step, arm in arm, we are creating a well-worn path of inspired vision and action, making mighty contributions, and offering our gifts in response to some of the world's greatest challenges. This is what our *kula* (community) does. But there is much more to do. Join us.

Join us and make a difference in the ways for which you have been uniquely destined. As you commit to caring for those who have been disregarded and forgotten by many, your life will glow in the darkness, your joy will be immeasurable, and your purpose on the planet will be as clear as day. You will live your life ablaze.

Visit bit.ly/SeedsComm to sign up for stories
from around the world that inspire
and ignite.
seedsofexchange.org | connect@seedsofexchange.org
Facebook and Instagram @SeedsOfExchange

Grateful

Thankful for Bran. Wow. Wow. I'm so wholly grateFULL for you, B-dawg! What a gift to have you with me as I wrote the first draft of this book. How I loved that! Soph and Micah, you've grown up with a momma who has a great passion for you *and* passions for other people and places in the world too. It takes a lot to share your momma, to create a rhythm as a family that works and feels good. Grateful for the support of my parents, Momma Sue, and Nana (how I miss you, Nana!), my sisters Beks and Liz, Aunts Deb and Pamela and your families; Vashti and Brahmers; Cody, Mel, Trae, and Brody; and the Carlson clan. For my sisters and brothers for life: Raq, Roch, Kat, Lis, and Erin; Marqui; Fatouma, Rose, Godee, and Marcellina; and the Cleveland, Callahan, Brady, Hecox, Wall, Boyer, Stenson, and Yondorf families. Thankful for the team that has been placed in my lap from My Word Publishing: Donna M., Andrea, Donna C., Susie, and Polly. For Yeshoda, who offered immeasurable help in my cultural and linguistic understanding of Nepal. For the Bhatta family and Vaun. For Astrid, Amy, and Veronica. For Grant's tenacious heart and commitment to craft *Untouchable: Children of God*, the extraordinary film that connected me with Hannah and her sisters … and essentially started this storytelling adventure. For Tom,

Rachael and Datta, Del, Amara, and the Groover Tribe. For this storytelling tool that allows us to connect, from anywhere in the world. For the stage this can be for my sisters in Nepal and India. Grateful for a body that is strong, pain-free, and healthy. For good food and plenty around me in my life. Dang! What a list. What gifts. A thing of beauty, to be sure.

Other Books
by Sarah Davison-Tracy

**BE Beloved: An Intimate,
Extraordinary Journey with Jesus**

BE Beloved has been structured to meet you in the midst of your daily life. Through Jesus' words spoken directly to you, and with Scripture woven throughout, the 40-BEs will guide you to *arrive* just as you are, *bask* in the words of Jesus meant just for you, *pray* with Jesus about what matters most to you, *savor* and *listen* to Scripture and music, *ponder* what is capturing your attention, and *prACTice* actions fueled by Jesus' love and companionship.

BE Beloved may quiet, console, and fill you with peace on one day and on another, ignite you and your reason for being. Whether or not you've lived knowing you are wholly loved by Jesus, allow this journey to draw you into rhythms of quiet communion and intentional action—knowing that the One who loves you is with you always. **Come as you are. Sit and be with Jesus.**

Soulfully Ablaze: A 40-Day Journey to Light Up Your Life (And the World)

This adventure will unleash within you a new vision for your unique ways to be a vital part of the lives of those who matter most to you in your family, neighborhood, and in far-flung parts of the world. It will amplify your purpose on the planet and help you cultivate a tribe of people that will delight and surprise you. It will fan the flame of your dormant or blazing dreams.

The timeframe of forty days is rooted in the power of both the spiritual and scientific to notably reframe, restart, and regenerate. Each day includes a reading for soulful learning and inspiration, followed by a time of simple stillness, reflection, and nudges for unique-to-you inspired action. You will have opportunities to weave these practices with ease into more bits of your life in ways that will create plentiful peace, flourishing freedom, herculean hope, and limitless love. One day at a time, your life will begin to light up with an unmistakable glow. This is where the fire of your life is stoked.

Live Ablaze: And Light Up the World

If you've ever wondered how one person could possibly make a difference just by showing up exactly as they are, you're in the right place. Welcome.

Sarah Davison-Tracy takes you on a guided and experiential journey that is both intimate and expansive, fueling you for a life that is peace-making, bridge-building, and change-making. One step at a time, get ready to uncover more of who you are and what matters most to you.

You may feel more than ready, eager to receive this journey's invitation, or you may feel a bit hesitant, especially if life seems overwhelming. Wherever you find yourself today, don't wait another moment. It's time to begin. Rather than another "to-do" in your life, Live Ablaze offers a pathway to connect with who you are and why you are here. As you explore, the glow of hope, peace, and love will stoke the flames of a life far beyond what you ever dared to dream.

About the Author

Whether traveling the globe or nestled in the backyard of her home in Colorado with her renaissance-man of a husband and two beloved children, Sarah Davison-Tracy is an impassioned human rights advocate, author, speaker, founder of Seeds of Exchange (SeedsofExchange.org) and Rooted and Beloved (RootedandBeloved.org).

Sarah seeks to ignite fierce love, connection, and justice so the people of the world are fueled by an unstoppable commitment to the well-being of one another. She believes with all her heart that she is on the planet to love. To love God and to love her sisters and brothers. To be love and to be loved. Unabashedly and unequivocally.

Having published four books, including *Live Ablaze: And Light Up the World*; *Soulfully Ablaze: A 40-Day Journey to Light Up Your Life (And the World)*; *BE Beloved: An Intimate, Extraordinary Journey with Jesus*; and *No Longer Untouchable: A Story of Human Trafficking, Heroism, and Hope*, no doubt she is, at this very moment, dreaming and scheming about her next tale to tell. Pop on over to connect with Sarah and explore what she is up to right here: SarahDavisonTracy.org.

Ten percent of book royalties are donated to the global change-making partners of Seeds of Exchange.

More Praise for
No Longer Untouchable

"It's important that Sarah Davison-Tracy has collected these testimonies and is making them available to the public. Listening to the stories of victims is an essential part of their healing as well as providing the impetus for societal change."

–3 Generations

"Gut-wrenching, heart-aching, and inspiring. You just can't get these stories out of your mind. A book that will call you to action and motivate you to stand up for justice."

–Andrea Costantine, Author of
*Connected: 101 Ways to Be of Service and
Create Community*

"Sarah, the great storyteller, the inspirer of minds and masses, an amazing human being, and a great sister to every woman who needs her, has narrated the heart-wrenching reality of the *Badi* community in Nepal in a way that makes you never want to sleep. How could you, when such shameful acts of inhumanity occur in your own neighborhood?

"A must-read book for everyone who feels any sense of responsibility for making this world a better and safer place for women."

—Jaimala Gupta, Co-Founder of Vatsalya
and Founder of Anoothi India

"Human trafficking as an everyday, real issue literally came across my desk in 2008, in the form of a *Social Worker Today* magazine cover. It left me aghast, sick to my stomach, and too traumatized to even read the full article. I had to put it aside. The topic continued to haunt me, but it was too painful for me to engage with this issue, especially as the mother of a young girl.

"Fast forward to 2015: Sarah Davison-Tracy invited me to meet Hannah, Raju, Sangita, Håkan, and the other Nepali team members staying with her. Because I have been friends with Sarah for twenty years, and because she spoke with so much excitement and love about these dear people, I was able to move through my secondary trauma and build relationships with these extraordinary people. It was not painful or heavy, but rather a joyful experience that completely transformed my ability to engage with the topic of human trafficking. The reason is that the beauty, power, and joy of all of these survivors who are thriving was a powerful revelation of restoration, resiliency, and the triumph of the human spirit. The passion and tireless advocacy with which Raju, Sangeeta, and Håkan love, serve, educate, and nourish the youth of Nepal is inspirational to me every time I think of this issue that exists around the world. *No Longer Untouchable* is a story of hope, strength, and encouragement that fuels me to act by doing what I can with what I have to give."

—Lisa Sharpe,
Founder of Stylish Sparrow

"A truly unforgettable book. The stories of these women will stick with you and be forever etched in your heart. Ambitious and artful storytelling at its best! *No Longer Untouchable* leaves the reader transformed and invites everyone to be a part of the change that is yet to be made. Bravo to the *No Longer Untouchable* storytelling team!"

–Rachael Jayne Groover,
Author of *Powerful and Feminine*
and *Divine Breadcrumbs*

"*No Longer Untouchable* is no ordinary book. The five heroines, and their true stories of moving from victims of human trafficking to active changemakers, will touch your heart and leave you thirsting to make a difference. In compiling their stories, Davison-Tracy has done a service to the world."

–Delta Donohue,
Author of *The First Taste Belongs to the Gods* and
Glancing Through the Rear View: A Year in Poetry

"Sarah Davison-Tracy and these extraordinary storytellers take readers on an unbelievable journey into the terrifying and oppressive world of sex trafficking. I am blown away by the courage of these women and their willingness to shed light on a huge atrocity in our world. Thank you all for bringing the shadow to the surface for deeper healing."

–Suzanne Hanna,
Founder and CEO of Global
Healing Collective and The Wilderness Walk

"Riveting from the start. Within the first three pages, I was already wondering how we live in the same world. How can I live on the same planet as the women who experienced what they did? How can my daughter? This is a heart-warming and eye-opening account of how the world can work, and what is possible when we come together and do something."

–Angela Melfi,
Founder and CEO of Threads Worldwide

"Sarah Davison-Tracy is a true storyteller by converting what is real into an impactful tale, where she presents this epic story to educate the public on what is happening to women and young girls out there. This sex trafficking narrative is a must-read book, as it takes you through the guiles that are adopted to buy these innocent and beautiful girls from Nepal and India into activities they never bargained for. This could happen to any one of us, and for Sarah to reveal this truth through this educational piece, is impeccable. The revelations in *No Longer Untouchable* will stick with you forever and will enlighten you to be watchful!"

–Evans Kwesi Mensah,
Consultant, Social Advocate,
and Author of *Synergy and Commonality:
The Key to Success* and *Beyond The Credentials.!?*

"Human trafficking is one of the most abhorrent practices occurring across the globe today, and yet it is all too easy to separate the story from the broken system, dehumanize it so we can move it out of our minds. Sarah Davison-Tracy has illuminated stories of women from the *Badi* community in Nepal to highlight the impact human trafficking has on individuals, families, and communities. *No Longer Untouchable* is a powerful story, written with compassion, devotion, and intention."

–Winter Wall,
Founder and CEO of W3 Global Consulting

"True stories, albeit painfully read, increase our ability to understand a person's trauma and motivate us to actively engage in advocacy work dedicated to a human rights-based approach. Human trafficking is a worldwide tortuous epidemic with lives often completely shattered by modern-day slavery. Only by bringing global awareness to local levels can we ever expect to end this horrific human crisis."

–Susanne E. Jalbert, Chief of Party for
USAID Promote: Women in Government

"A must-read for anyone who wants to truly hear the voices of five extraordinary women who were once silent and invisible sex trafficked slaves."

–Gayle Nosal,
Director of NeeNee Productions